kiddiwalks in Oxfordshire

Ruth Paley

COUNTRYSIDE BOOKS
NEWBURY BERKSHIRE

First published 2012
© Ruth Paley 2012

COUNTRYSIDE BOOKS
3 Catherine Road
Newbury, Berkshire

To view our complete range of books,
please visit us at
www.countrysidebooks.co.uk

ISBN 978 1 84674 283 5

For Tabatha and Lola

Designed by Peter Davies, Nautilus Design
Produced through MRM Associates Ltd., Reading
Printed by Information Press, Oxford

Contents

Contents

PUBLISHER'S NOTE

We hope that you obtain considerable enjoyment from this book; great care has been taken in its preparation. Although at the time of publication all routes followed public rights of way or permitted paths, diversion orders can be made and permissions withdrawn.

We cannot, of course, be held responsible for such diversion orders and any inaccuracies in the text which result from these or any other changes to the routes nor any damage which might result from walkers trespassing on private property. We are anxious though that all details covering the walks are kept up to date and would therefore welcome information from readers which would be relevant to future editions.

The simple sketch maps that accompany the walks in this book are based on notes made by the author whilst checking out the routes on the ground. They are designed to show you how to reach the start, to point out the main features of the overall circuit and they contain a progression of numbers that relate to the paragraphs of the text.

However, for the benefit of a proper map, we do recommend that you purchase the relevant Ordnance Survey sheet covering your walk. The Ordnance Survey maps are widely available, especially through booksellers and local newsagents.

Introduction

These 20 walks have been carefully chosen to provide a variety of interesting days out, that will appeal to children, and their parents. The walks are shorter than those in a traditional walking book, as a child's pace is slower than an adult's, and is punctuated with stops to explore a stream, climb a tree, or for a quick snack. The idea is to encourage children to see walking as a fun adventure and nurture a hobby that they can enjoy throughout their lives. Walking is a free activity that connects you to nature and the surrounding countryside.

Each walk has a *Fun Things to See and Do* section, which is aimed specifically at children. This offers ideas on being a nature detective, telling children about the birds and animals they might see on the walk, mentions nearby play areas for younger children or tells older children of spooky folk tales or legends linked to the site. The *Background Notes* suggest other places to visit nearby, or give information on the history, geology or wildlife of the area.

Oxfordshire is the perfect county in which to foster a lifelong love of walking. Few counties in England can boast such a variety of stunning countryside. From rolling farmland in the north, you can explore Cotswold's green valleys and the magnificent bluebell woods at Foxholes and Badbury Hill in the west. In the east, are the downland hills and beechwoods of the Chilterns, which surround the 16th-century Greys Court manor house, while the south of the county reaches down to the ancient landscape of the Vale of the White Horse, crossed by the prehistoric Ridgeway national path.

On these walks, children can connect with history as they explore an Iron Age fort at Uffington, the site of England's oldest chalk-cut hill figure; visit the remains of a large Roman villa near North Leigh; or wonder at the mysterious Rollright Stones, by Chipping Norton. A walk through Oxford invites children to look up at the gargoyles and grotesques, peering down from the walls around them. Nature reserves make for perfect family walking, and Chimney Meadows in the south is an idyllic spot. For birdwatchers, the RSPB reserve at Otmoor is not to be missed, while from Watlington Hill in the Chilterns, you can watch the red kite swoop and soar in the sky around you.

Kiddiwalks in Oxfordshire

I would like to thank my three wonderful children aged 11, 9 and 7, who have enthusiastically tested every walk in this book, stopping along the way for many picnics on fallen tree trunks or by the corner of a field, and my husband, Matt, for carrying the many picnics.

Ruth Paley

AREA MAP SHOWING THE LOCATIONS OF THE WALKS

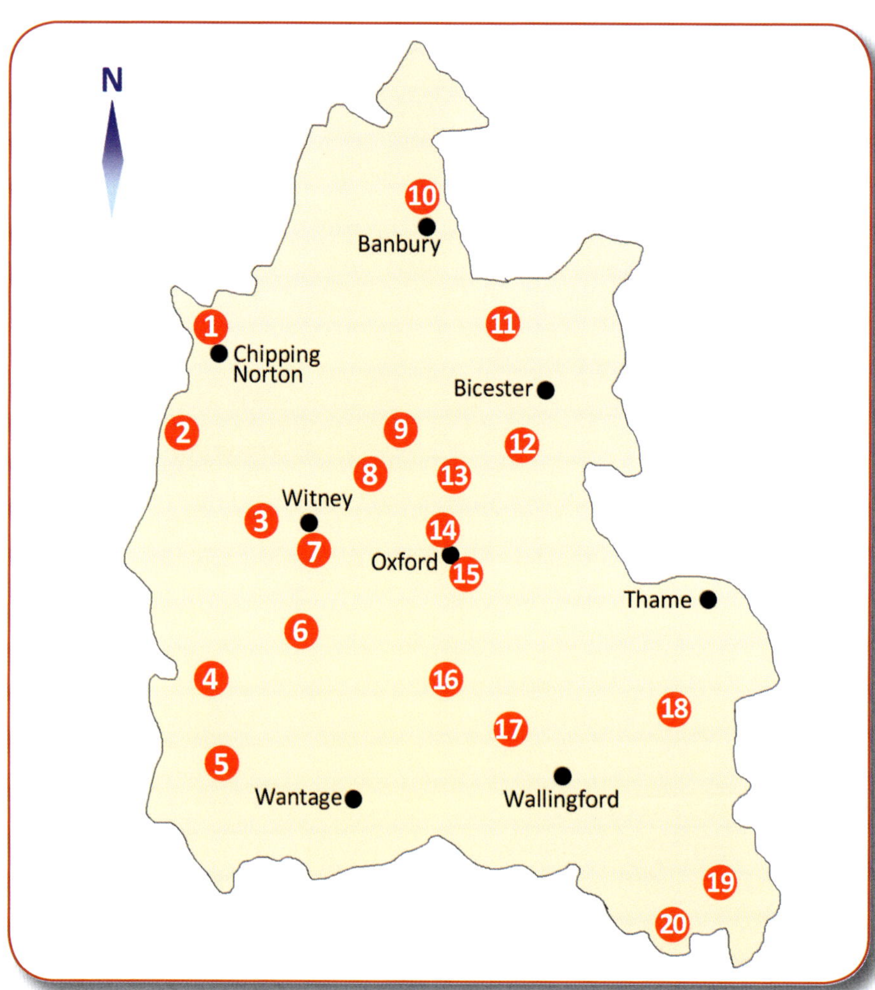

The Rollright Stones

A Petrified King and his Courtiers

A walk with panoramic views over rolling farmland leads you to the Rollright Stones. These ancient megaliths are on three sites, the solitary King Stone, the King's Men stone circle and the Whispering Knights burial chamber. After exploring the stones, the walk meanders through fields of sheep and a copse to return to the hamlet of Little Rollright.

Kiddiwalks in Oxfordshire

Getting there Little Rollright is about 4 miles north-west of Chipping Norton. Heading north along the A3400, take the left turn, signed 'Rollright Stones'. Then take the first left after the stones and follow the signs for Little Rollright. Drive slowly through the village as the roads are not well surfaced and the area is popular with walkers. The road to the church is signed.

Length of walk 3 miles
Time 2 hours
Terrain Field paths with some uphill sections, stiles and kissing gates. Not suitable for buggies or dogs.
Start/Parking There is a free car park by the church in Little Rollright (GR SP295301).
Map OS Explorer 191 Banbury, Bicester & Chipping Norton
Refreshments Wyatts Farm Shop and Tea Room is 1 mile east of the stones near Great

Standing in the King's Men circle.

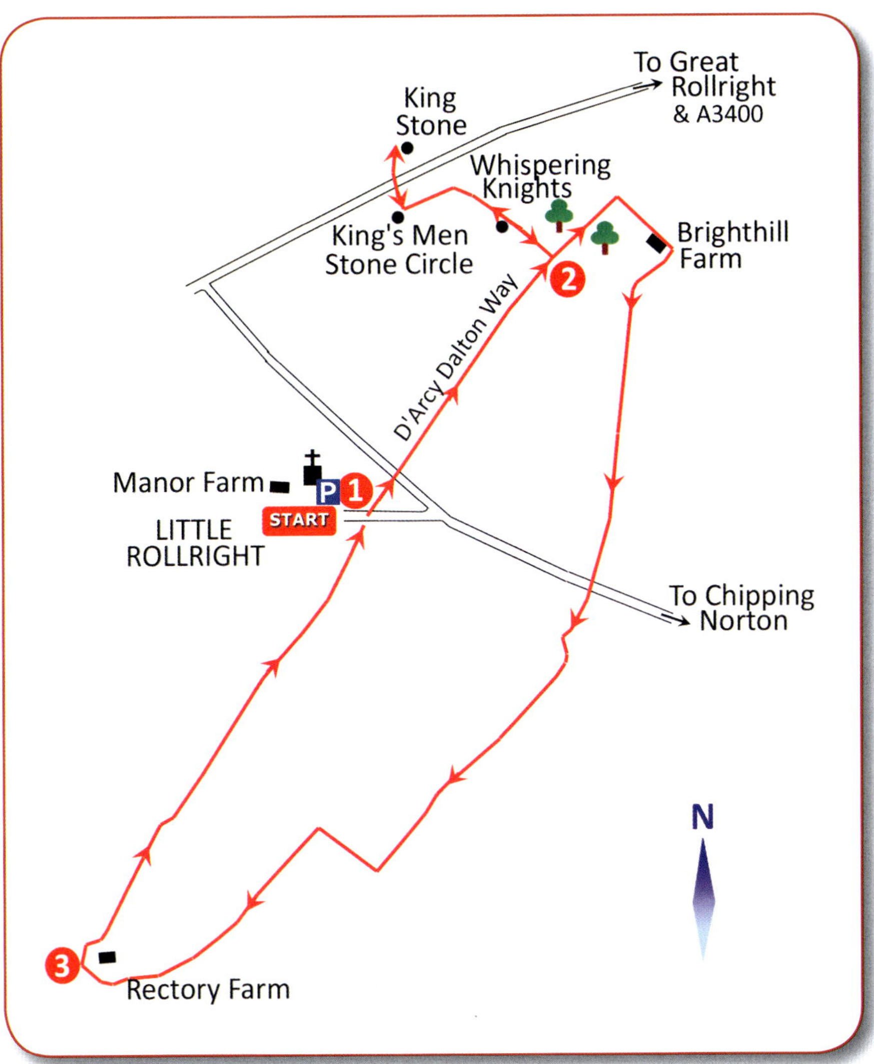

Rollright. They sell home-made ice cream, cakes and bread. The grassy area around the Rollright Stones is a perfect picnic spot.

The Walk

1 Follow the road back the way you came, heading away from the

◆ Fun Things to See and Do ◆

Legends say that a local king and his army met a witch in this field. She turned the army into the stone circle of King's Men. The King Stone across the road is the king himself and the Whispering Knights are four of his knights, petrified as they leant together, plotting against their king. Younger children could count how many soldiers they can see in the circle of King's Men. Look for faces in the stones, some of them seem to be huddled together, others could be wearing cloaks.

Older children could **explore the lichen** on the stones. Lichen grows very slowly, sometimes only half a millimetre a year. Although these plants are not as old as the ancient stones they grow on, some of the lichen is up to 800 years old. Look at all sides of the stones and see if the lichen growing in the sun is different from the lichen in the shade. There are around 1,700 species of lichen in Britain, many of which only grow in a certain spot.

Manor House for about 40 yards, until you come to a footpath sign on your left to the 'Rollright Stones via D'Arcy Dalton Way'. Follow this path gently uphill, passing through two kissing gates. When you come to a road, cross it with care and continue ahead along the footpath, over the fields. This stretch of the walk has beautiful views back to the church and the surrounding farmland. Shortly, you will see the Whispering Knights on your left and some trees ahead of you.

2 You will return to this spot to continue the walk after visiting the stones. There is a permissive footpath leading round the field. Turn left and walk up to the Whispering Knights. Then continue along this path, turning left at the edge of the field for about 250 yards to find the King's Men circle. This is where the warden sits so make sure you have some change ready. The King Stone is on the other side of the road. When you have finished at the site, retrace your steps, past the Whispering Knights to return to the original footpath. Turn left and cross two stiles to continue along the D'Arcy Dalton Way for a short, shady stretch through a private wood. Cross the stile, then turn right onto a public footpath that leads you past Brighthill Farm. Cross the stile into a field and walk diagonally right, downhill to a gate in the corner. Follow the edge of the next field, passing a pond at the bottom to go through a metal gate. Turn right and walk beside a large field and through a metal gate to another field. There should be a gap in the crops where the footpath leads straight across this field. At the other side of the field, cross the road and follow the bridleway straight on. You will see the steeple of Little Rollright church to your right. The path veers left at the bottom of the field. Here, take a right turn, through a gap in the hedge. Cross the field ahead of you. Turn right at the edge of the field to the corner and go left through a gap by a wooden gate. Continue ahead along a bridleway and cross two fields. You will see the occasional sign on your left for Salford Trout Lakes. Continue ahead, passing Rectory Farm on your right.

3 Just past the farm gates, turn right to rejoin the D'Arcy Dalton Way. After about 10 yards, follow the sign to the right, over a stile, and veer left across the field to another stile, with Rectory Farm on your right. Cross the stile and continue ahead with a copse on your right. Look out for a stile on your right and turn into the wood. The path leads through the wood and across a field for a short distance to a gate on the right. Go through the gate and turn left to cross a stile by a brook. Walk gently uphill through a conifer wood to a field, where you continue ahead on the footpath. Go through two kissing gates to a narrow path between two fields, bordered with wild flowers in summer. This leads you down to a farm track by the edge of Little Rollright. Continue ahead to your car.

◆ Background Notes ◆

The **Rollright Stones** date from around 3,500 BC to 1,500 BC and span the Neolithic and Bronze Age. The site is owned by the Rollright Trust which has a warden to collect the admission charge of £1 per adult and 50p per child over 7 years of age. There are boards at each site providing information about the history of the stones and past excavations.

Foxholes Nature Reserve
Carpets of Bluebells, Bats and Birdsong

Benches are dotted along the route.

This tranquil woodland was once part of the ancient Wychwood Forest. It is one of Oxfordshire's best bluebell woods and, in May, the flowers are spectacular. In summer, you can see the spikes of tall foxgloves, spot the five different species of orchid and watch the many butterflies, while in autumn, over 200 types of fungus poke out from the thick carpet of autumn leaves. This walk follows part of the Wildlife Walk through the nature reserve, then returns via a grassy footpath across Fifield Heath.

> **Getting there** Take the A424 north out of Burford. After 3 miles, take the right turn to Bruern. Continue ahead past a staggered crossroads and stay on this road for 2 miles. Pass a right turn for Shipton-under-Wychwood, then after about 300 yards, look out for a narrow rutted track which leads for about 500 yards to a small BBOWT free car park. This track is very uneven and potholed, though, and you are strongly recommended to park on the grass verge at the start of the track and walk down it to start the walk rather than carry on to the car park. The track can also be accessed from the north-west by following the B4450 to the hamlet of Foscot. The track is on your left as you head south through the hamlet.

Length of walk 1½ miles
Time 1½ hours
Terrain Unsurfaced woodland paths and fields with some stiles. Muddy after rain.
Start/Parking Park on the grass verge at the southern end of the track and walk down the track to start the walk. (GR SP258208).
Map OS Explorer OL45 The Cotswolds
Refreshments Burford High Street has lots of tempting delicatessens and tea rooms. There are benches at Foxholes for picnics.

The Walk

1 From the car park, cross the track and take the grassy path in front of you, passing Brock Cottage on your right. Go through a kissing gate and continue ahead until you come to a post, where the path forks. Go through the wooden barrier into the nature reserve and follow the Wildlife Walk. This runs parallel to the bridleway, which you will be able to see on your left. Pass an information board about bats and look up to see lots of bat boxes fixed to the trees. At the end of the path, go through a wooden barrier to re-join the bridleway, and turn right.

2 After a short while, you reach a bench in front of a staggered gate. Go through the gate and follow the Wildlife Walk, passing another bench on your right and more bat boxes on your left. Ignore a permissive footpath on your right and continue ahead. Stay on the Wildlife Walk, passing a boardwalk on your right and blackberry bushes on your left.

At the end of this path, turn left along a short boardwalk and follow the path through the woods, heading north-east. Stay on this path, passing a signpost on your left then a little further along a bench on your right, made from the trunk of a fallen oak tree. Go through a wooden barrier to meet a path with a post in front of you.

◆ Fun Things to See and Do ◆

The Wildlife Trust is helping the **bats** by fixing bat boxes to the trees. See how many boxes you can spot as you walk round the woods. In spring, listen out for drumming **woodpeckers** above you. This is how the male woodpecker lets all the other woodpeckers know that this is his territory. He makes the sound by tapping his beak very quickly against a tree trunk. There are also barn owls, little owls and tree creepers in the woods.

3 Now leave the Wildlife Walk and turn right, following a bridleway to a field. Turn left and walk by the edge of the field for about 10 yards, then follow the path ahead into the trees. Walk through this strip of woodland and veer right, heading for a stile with a public footpath sign by it. Cross the

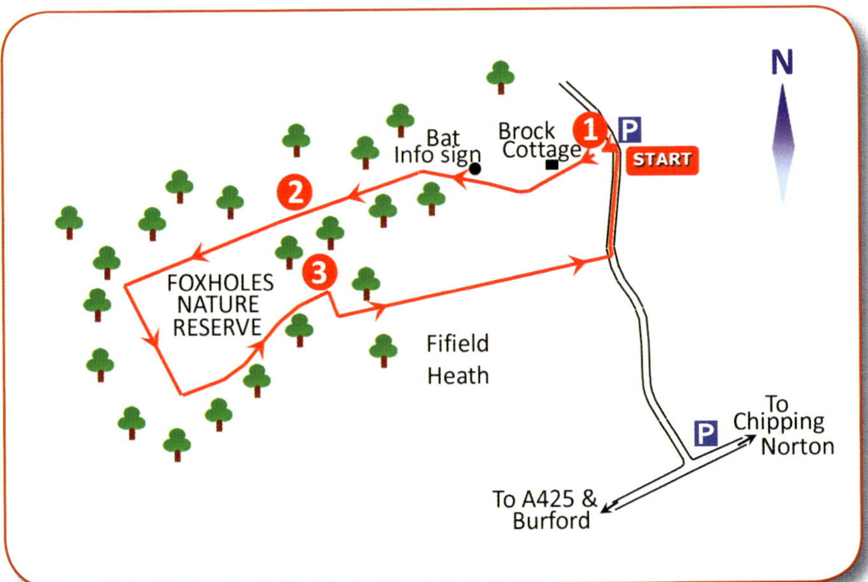

stile and walk straight ahead, following the right edge of the field to another stile. Cross it and continue across the next field and stile to the track. Now, depending on where you are parked, turn left to the car park, or right to the grass verge.

◆ Background Notes ◆

Bluebells thrive in a woodland habitat, where the fallen leaves act as an insulator, raising the ground temperature. The leaves also produce heat as they break down. This encourages the bulbs to grow and flower, enabling the bluebells to complete their life cycle in spring, before the trees come into full leaf and while light levels are high.

Seven different types of **bat** live at Foxholes, including the rare Bechstein's bat. Bats eat insects and they catch them by making very high pitched sounds as they fly. This creates a sound wave which goes through the air, bounces back off the insect and returns to the bat. The bat can then work out where the insect is, as well as how big and how far away it is. A bat's 'voice' is so high that adults can't hear it, they have to use a special bat detector, but some lucky children can hear the bats if they listen very carefully. Bats are most active at night, dusk and dawn, when lots of tasty insects are also flying around the woods. They spend most of their day hanging upside down in caves, hollowed-out trees or bat boxes. Bats are very sociable and like to live in a colony. They are mammals, like us, and have lived on the earth for more than 50 million years.

The Cotswold town of **Burford** is one of the prettiest towns in Oxfordshire. The shops on the High Street are all built from Cotswold stone, with gift shops and a traditional sweet shop to tempt children. Tolsey Museum, on the High Street, is free to visit and provides an insight into the town's social and industrial past. It also has an exquisite doll's house, furnished in the style of the Jane Austen period. It is open in the afternoons from April to October.

Minster Lovell Hall

Manor House Ruins in the Windrush Valley

Admiring the lambs.

The Cotswolds is the largest designated 'Area of Outstanding Natural Beauty' in England and most of the countryside is given over to farming. The distinctive honey-coloured limestone which makes Cotswold towns and villages so beautiful has been quarried here since Roman times. This walk crosses fields to the village of Crawley before returning by the side of the River Windrush, with beautiful views across the Cotswold landscape. You then have a chance to explore the striking ruins of the 15th-century Minster Lovell hall and dovecote.

3

Getting there Head west for 3 miles from Witney along the A40 or B4047. Minster Lovell Hall is signed and is at the north-eastern end of the village.

Length of walk 3 miles
Time 2½ hours
Terrain A small stretch of road without pavement. Some stiles and slopes, fields and woodland paths.
Start/Parking Free car park at the north-eastern end of Minster Lovell village, near the church and hall (GR SP325114).
Map OS Explorer 180 Oxford, Witney & Woodstock
Refreshments The Lamb pub in Crawley welcomes children and has a paved seating area outside. (☎ 01993 703753)

The Walk

1 From the car park, turn right and walk out of the village, following the sign for Crawley. Ignore a footpath sign on your left by a 30 mph sign and take the right turn past the national speed limit sign, to follow the Crawley Circular Walk footpath. Go through a kissing gate and walk across the field and through the gate opposite, with a small stream on either side. Walk across

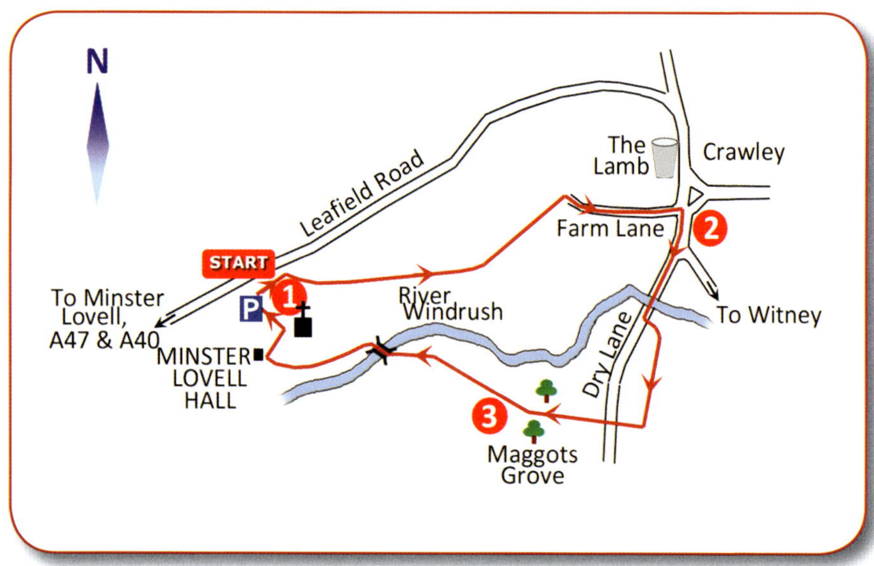

◆ Fun Things to See and Do ◆

The lush green meadows of the Cotswolds are ideal for **sheep farming** and in spring, children will delight in watching **new-born lambs** gambolling in the fields. The native sheep is the Cotswold Lion, prized for its long, heavy fleece. By the beginning of the 20th century, there were only a few flocks of this breed left. However, through the work of conservationists, there are now more than 50 flocks nibbling the green grass of the Cotswolds.

At the end of the walk, younger children can use their imaginations as they play at being kings, queens and knights in the **ruins of Minster Lovell Hall**. The ruins have large information panels by them for older children to work out what they are looking at and discover the history of the site.

the next field with a fence on your left. You can see the Crawley Mill chimney ahead of you. Go through a kissing gate and continue along the path, heading first uphill, then down to a stile. Continue ahead as the path winds uphill again with hedges on either side, until you come to the edge of Crawley. Turn right along Farm Lane. There is no pavement here, but the cul-de-sac is very quiet. There is a lovely view on your right across the valley and the River Windrush. Reach a junction at the bottom of the road, with the Lamb pub on your left.

2 Turn right and walk on the pavement along Dry Lane, past Manor Farm and a stream on your right. Go over the humpback bridge then cross the road with care. Walk along the grass verge for a few yards then take the bridleway on the left signed to Witney. This is a very pretty stretch of the walk, with a stream on the left and sheep in the fields on the right. When you come to gates, turn right, following the circular walk arrow. Walk uphill by the edge of a field, with a view of the mill chimney on your right. Cross the road and follow the bridleway ahead of you, going

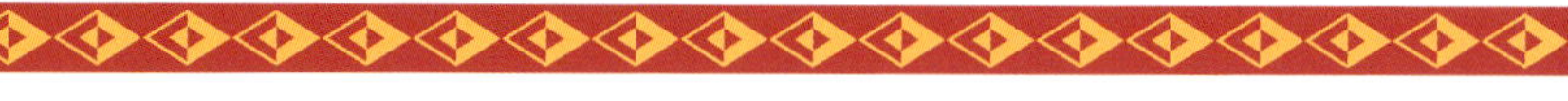

through a kissing gate, to walk across the field and through another kissing gate into Maggots Grove.

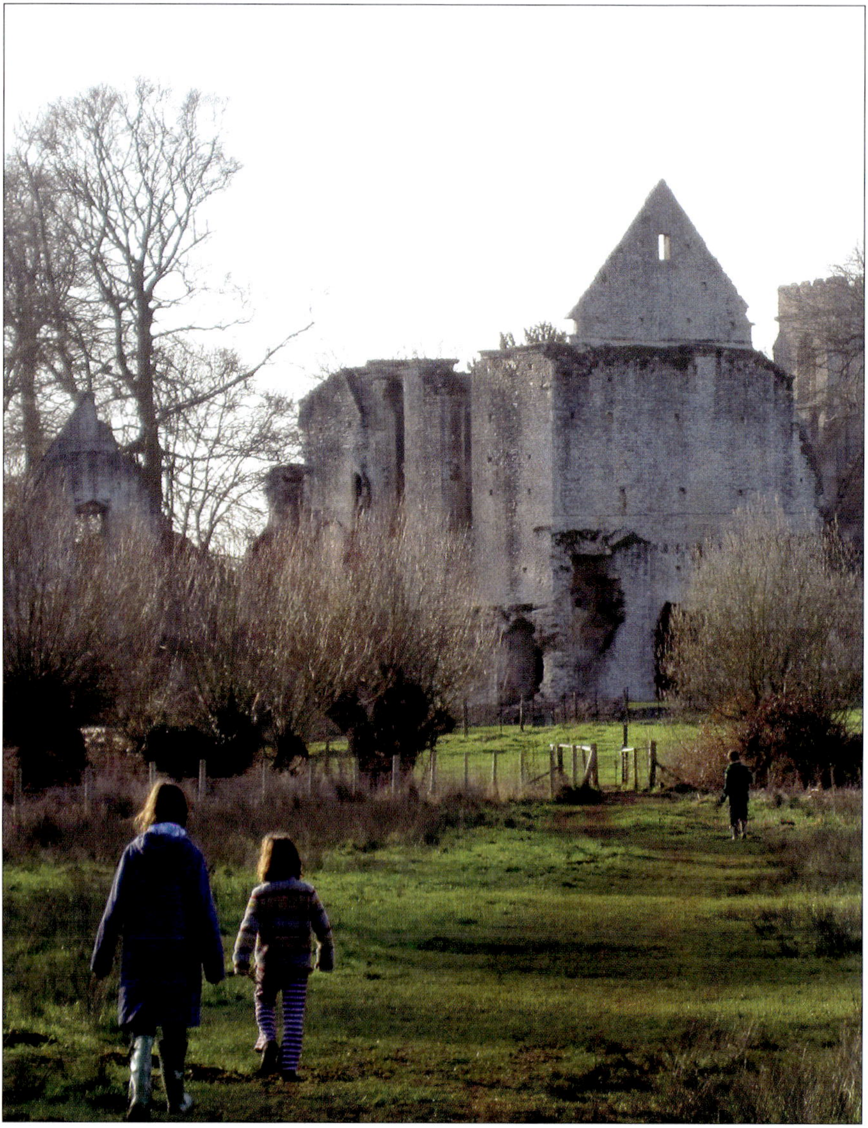

The ruins of Minster Lovell Hall.

3 Follow the path downhill to a farm gate. Go through the gate and walk across the field, with the River Windrush on your right. Go through another kissing gate and continue across the field to a stile, which takes you very close to the River Windrush. Walk across the next field and go through a kissing gate into conifer trees. Take the right turn to cross two small footbridges and walk with the water on your right.

Cross a narrow footbridge over the river and you will see the ruins of Minster Lovell Hall on the horizon. Continue ahead across the field to the ruins then walk across the churchyard to a narrow road. No cars are allowed on this road so don't worry about the lack of pavements. Turn left and walk along this road to the car park. Turn left at the car park if you want to explore the stone cottages and gardens of Minster Lovell village.

◆ Background Notes ◆

At the end of this walk, you see the ruins of **Minster Lovell Hall**, tower and dovecote silhouetted against the sky before you. William Lovell built the manor house in the 1420s. However, the family fortunes turned when William's grandson, Francis Lovell, sided with his childhood friend, Richard III of the House of York, during the Wars of the Roses. At the Battle of Bosworth Field, in 1485, Richard lost his life and his throne to Henry Tudor, of the House of Lancaster. Francis Lovell was charged with treason and was forced to flee the country, while Minster Lovell Hall was seized by the Crown and given to Jasper Tudor, uncle of the new King Henry VII. Lovell returned for a final attempt to dethrone Henry, when he led the rebel army at the Battle of Stoke, in 1487. What became of Francis Lovell after this is shrouded in mystery. Some tales say that he died in the battle, others that he fled to Minster Lovell, where he hid in a vaulted underground room and slowly starved to death. Builders broke into the room in 1708 and found a skeleton, sitting at a table with some papers. The skeleton and papers crumbled to dust in the cold air. This is a good, if rather gruesome ending to the story. However, as the house belonged to the House of Lancaster after the battle, it was not the most obvious place for Lovell to have sought refuge.

Badbury Clump

Iron Age Hill Fort Carpeted with Bluebells

These woods are owned by the National Trust and form part of the Buscot and Coleshill estate. Under Badbury Hill's beech trees lie the earthen ramparts and ditch of an Iron Age hill fort, built around 2,500 years ago. In spring, this ground is transformed by a carpet of bluebells. Coxwell Wood is a pretty mix of conifers and native broadleaf trees, with views to the west across gently rolling farmland. The walk leaves the woods to follow a short stretch of the D'Arcy Dalton Way, passing through two farms, before heading back across the fields to the woods. On this walk it would be useful to bring a compass with you to check you are walking in the right direction through the woods.

Length of walk 3½ miles
Time 3 hours
Terrain Unsurfaced paths through the woods and bridleways. Some steep uphill sections and a few stiles.
Start/Parking The free National Trust car park at the start of the walk (GR SU263946).
Map OS Explorer 170 Abingdon, Wantage & Vale of White Horse
Refreshments The Radnor Arms (☎ 01793 861575) is 1½ miles west in Coleshill. It serves excellent food and has a picturesque beer garden and children's play area. Alternatively, sit by the edge of the woods for a picnic. There may also be an ice cream van in the car park during the summer.

The Walk

1 There is a map at the end of the car park and some information about the woods. Go through the gate next to the map and Badbury Hill is directly in front of you. It looks like a hot cross bun on the map with footpaths that take you through the bluebells, in season. Follow the wide path ahead for about 50 yards, before turning left along a small path. This leads you to a footpath with a National Trust sign and a road on your left. Turn right to follow the path through the western edge of the woods. Shortly you will begin to glimpse the fields through the trees on your left. There are two benches with a wonderful view across the farmland. Ignore any tracks on your left or right, until you come to a T-junction. Turn left and walk downhill a short distance towards the edge of the wood, then veer right as the path winds through the trees, with blackberry bushes on your right.

2 When you come to a public footpath which crosses your route, with a disused stile and two yellow footpath arrows on your right, turn left and follow the footpath downhill and out of the woods to an arable field, passing a yellow footpath arrow on your right. Walk towards Brimstone Farm, which you will see directly ahead of you. At the edge of the field, turn left then almost immediately right to continue along the footpath over a small footbridge and across the next field. At the farmyard, turn right and walk past the outbuildings, keeping the farmhouse on your right. Take the path directly ahead of you, passing a D'Arcy Dalton Way arrow on your right. Walk along the track to Oldfield Farm, skirting to the left of the farm. Then leave the footpath to head east along a wide stony track to Rowleaze Cottages – traditional estate workers' cottages now owned by the National Trust.

3 Walk across the parking area, through a gate and ahead across the field. You reach a gate with two arrows, indicating a bridleway and public footpath. The footpath turns left here, but this walk follows the bridleway straight ahead to follow the edge of the field, with a small copse on your right. When you come to a T-junction with a wide grassy path, with Coxwell Wood on the horizon ahead of you, turn left and follow the path with fields either side. At the end of this path there is a wooden telegraph pole with a map of the area nailed to it. Turn right here then go over the stile with a blue bridleway arrow that you can see on your left. Follow the path through some trees and continue ahead by the field's edge until you come to a stile. From here you can see Wood House at the top of the hill on your left.

4 Cross the stile and follow a narrow woodland path uphill past blackberry bushes. The path ends at a wider path running from left to right. Turn right, shortly passing a path leading up on the left, and continue ahead. This

◆ Fun Things to See and Do ◆

As you walk across the fields, look out for the **beetle banks** on either side of the path. These long grassy strips have been left by the farmer to provide a winter habitat for insects, spiders, ground-nesting birds and small mammals, like harvest mice. This helps the wildlife and the farmer, as in spring, the beetles will crawl into the field and eat the bad bugs which attack the farmer's crop. The woods surrounding Badbury Hill are full of **blackberry bushes**, as well as **trees to climb** and fallen branches for **den building**.

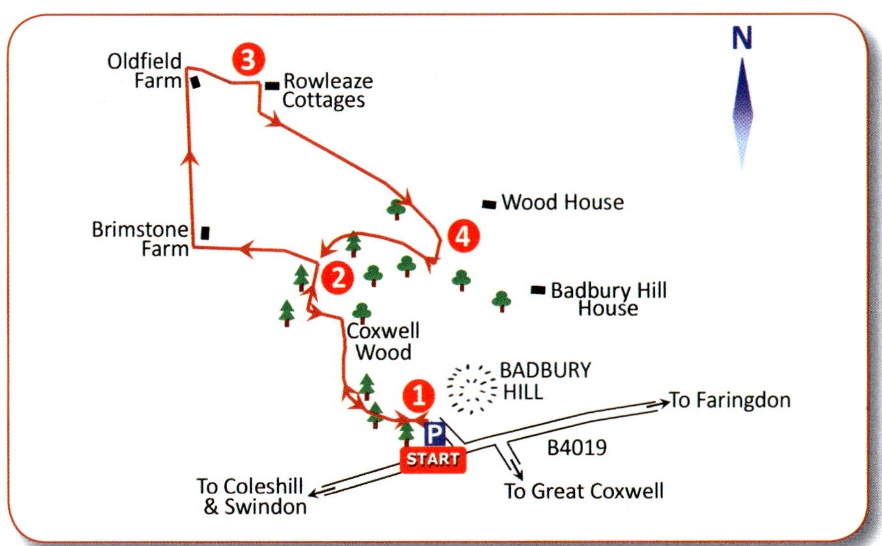

path soon passes the disused stile with two yellow arrows that you saw earlier. Continue ahead and retrace your steps. The path veers left and uphill to the T-junction, where you turn right and follow the path as it curves round the woods, passing the two benches. Continue ahead until you spot the road and National Trust sign ahead. Turn left along the narrow path and return to the car park.

◆ Background Notes ◆

William Morris used to bring his guests to nearby **Great Coxwell Barn** to admire its structure. The barn is open all year and is free to visit. About 1½ miles to the north is **Buscot Park** and grounds. The house is owned by the National Trust and has an impressive art collection, including Burne-Jones's *Legend of the Briar Rose*. This series of paintings stretches round the walls of the saloon and illustrates the story of Sleeping Beauty. Outside, children can look out for the seventeen life-size models of China's terracotta warriors, then stop for a rest in the Swinging Garden. Check opening times and admission prices by visiting www.buscotpark.com.

5

Uffington White Horse and Wayland's Smithy

Exploring Ancient Britain

This is a walk steeped in ancient history and folklore. It starts by exploring the enigmatic Uffington White Horse, carved into the chalk hillside around 3,000 years ago, during the Bronze Age, then visits the natural mound of Dragon Hill, the legendary spot where St George slew the dragon. The route then leads round the rampart ditches of Iron-Age Uffington Castle to join the Ridgeway. Follow this ancient path in the footsteps of prehistoric herdsmen and soldiers to the atmospheric Neolithic burial chamber of Wayland's Smithy. There is an option for younger families to shorten the walk.

Uffington White Horse and Wayland's Smithy

Getting there The turning for Uffington White Horse is on the B4507, just south of the village of Woolstone. Follow the brown tourist signs to the National Trust car park on your left.

Length of walk 3½ or 1½ miles
Time 3 hours or 1 hour
Terrain Some steep slopes, steps, gates and chalk paths with a small section of road walking. Suitable for all-terrain pushchairs.
Start/Parking The National Trust pay and display car park at Uffington White Horse. It is free for members, otherwise £2 for one hour and £3.50 for two to four hours (GR SU293866).
Map OS Explorer 170 Abingdon, Wantage & Vale of White Horse
Refreshments Sometimes there is an ice cream van in the car park, and the top of the hill by the White Horse is a perfect spot for a windy picnic, with a panoramic view across the downs. Alternatively, there are two beautiful 16th-century pubs nearby that both serve food, the White Horse Inn in Woolstone (☎ 01367 820726) and the Rose and Crown Inn in Ashbury (☎ 01793 710222).

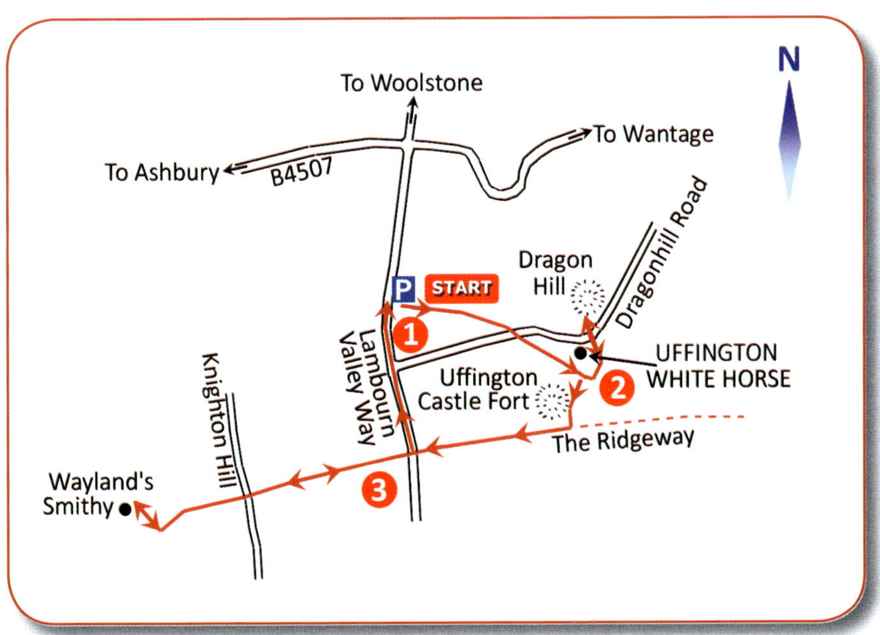

Kiddiwalks in Oxfordshire

5

◆ Fun Things to See and Do ◆

Children can let their imaginations run riot as they explore these ancient sites. The scoop of land directly below the horse is known as **The Manger**, which is where the white horse is said to graze at night. The ripples on its eastern side are the **Giant's Stairs**, formed during the last Ice Age. The image of a horse running across the downland can best be seen from the sky. Maybe it was made for the ancient sun god Belenos, who rode across the sky in a chariot pulled by horses? Legends say that St George killed the dragon on top of **Dragon Hill** and the white chalk scar is where he spilt the dragon's blood, poisoning the soil forever.

The Walk

1 Walk up the steps by the side of the car park and through a gate. Follow the sign that points the way up to the White Horse. As you walk up White Horse Hill, almost immediately there are fantastic views back across the rolling downland. When you come to Dragonhill Road, there is a wooden board on your left which explains the view, from Swindon in the east all the way across Oxfordshire to the Chilterns. Go through the gate and cross the road with care. The path then veers to the left and leads you up the hill from where you can see the sinuous lines of the chalk horse directly below you. You could take a detour to explore Dragon Hill, by walking down beside the horse to the road. Cross with care then walk up some steps to the top of Dragon Hill. When you have finished, retrace your steps back to the top of the horse.

2 Follow the path back for about 200 yards to a sign that you passed on the way up, pointing to Uffington Castle and the White Horse. This time turn left and follow a grassy path uphill past the huge ramparts of Uffington Castle and a trig point on your right. You will see the white chalk path of the Ridgeway in front of you. Go through the gate and turn right, heading gently downhill. The path passes a NT sign on the right for White

Uffington White Horse and Wayland's Smithy

Horse Hill, then levels out and passes through hedgerows and blackberry bushes to a crossroads. You could shorten the route by turning right here and following the sign for Woolstone back to the car park. Alternatively, continue along the Ridegeway to explore Wayland's Smithy, passing a NT map on your left.

At Wayland's Smithy.

3 Follow the path past fields and across a surfaced track, following the restricted byway sign. Shortly you will see a sign for Wayland's Smithy. To explore this atmospheric ancient site turn right through a gate and down a short footpath towards some tall beech trees. When you have finished, retrace your steps to the Ridgeway. Turn left and walk back along the track. Cross the surfaced road and continue to the next crossroads. Turn left and follow the surfaced track signed to Woolstone. This route is part of the Lambourn Valley Way. The car park is signed on your right.

◆ Background Notes ◆

Uffington White Horse was made in the Bronze Age by cutting trenches into the ground, then filling the trenches with chalk. It is the oldest chalk-cut hill figure in the country. **Uffington Castle** is an Iron Age hill fort, strategically positioned to guard the important trading route of the **Ridgeway**. For around 5,000 years, drovers, traders and soldiers walked along this prehistoric track as it crossed the country from Dorset to the Wash, in Norfolk. **Wayland's Smithy** is a Neolithic long barrow and is around 5,000 years old. A long earth mound and ditches were added around 2,800 BC. The entrance to the tomb was originally blocked by large sarsen stones and the remains of Neolithic people have been found at the site. Wayland was the Saxon god of metalworking. Folktales say that if you left a horse and a silver coin at the mound for a time, upon your return you would find the horse shod and the coin taken.

Chimney Meadows Nature Reserve
Wild Flowers and Water Birds

Chimney Meadows Nature Reserve is one of the country's largest areas of unspoilt grasslands. This tranquil walk explores its wildflower meadows and wetlands, by the banks of the River Thames. The walk passes two bird hides, giving children an opportunity to observe a variety of wetland birds, before crossing the Thames where you can stop on the bridge to watch the dragonflies and damselflies dancing over the water. Chimney Meadows is a beautiful nature reserve and you can do the whole walk without seeing a single car or house.

Chimney Meadows Nature Reserve

Getting there Chimney is 5 miles south of Witney. From the A415, take the turning for Aston. In the village, pass the turning for the B4449 and head south down Bull Lane Ditch for Chimney.

Length of walk 3 miles
Time 2 hours
Terrain Flat grassy paths which can get boggy in winter. BBOWT prefer no dogs in the Nature Reserve to protect the sensitive habitat and rare ground-breeding birds.
Start/Parking Free BBOWT car park on the left as you follow the single track to Chimney. The walk starts from the small footbridge into the field, opposite the car park (GR SP354013).
Map OS Explorer 180 Oxford
Refreshments The Trout Inn at Tadpole Bridge has a beautiful beer garden. The lunch menu includes children's meals (☎ 01367 870382). There are some picnic tables in the Nature Reserve.

The Walk

1 From the car park, cross the road and go over a small footbridge into a field. Turn left and follow the permissive footpath to the opposite end of this field. Cross the road and go through a metal gate into the Nature Reserve. Follow the path across the field to another metal gate. Go through the gate and turn right, following a permissive footpath round the edge of the field until you come to a gap in the hedge on your right and a footpath sign.

2 Follow the signs for the bird hide by going through the gate, then turning left and through another gate to follow a path with a hedgerow on your right. There

◆ Fun Things to See and Do ◆

On the walk you pass two **bird hides** where binoculars and large posters are available to help you to identify the birds. There is a notebook in the larger hide for you to record the birds you see. For younger children, the bridge halfway along the route is a good spot for playing **pooh sticks**, and there are blackberries to pick by the bridge in late summer.

is an information board here on your left. The field on your right is a sensitive conservation area where the Trust is creating an ideal habitat for birds and for the insects that you may hear buzzing and humming around you. At the end of the field, the path turns to the right and leads you past an owl box fixed to a tall tree, and the larger of the two bird hides. Follow the boardwalk through a wet grassland landscape, passing the smaller bird hide and weaving through trees to a gate.

3 Go through the gate and turn left along a surfaced bridleway. Cross a footbridge and pass some

picnic tables and an information board on your right. When you come to two gates, go through the wooden gate on your right, staying on the bridleway to cross a footbridge over the River Thames. Continue along this path for a short distance, through a wooden gate into a large meadow. Veer left for about 15 yards, heading for a wooden post and gap in the hedge, edged with wooden fencing. Then follow this permissive footpath until you come to a metal gate on your right.

4 Go through the gate, passing another information board on your left and walk across the field,

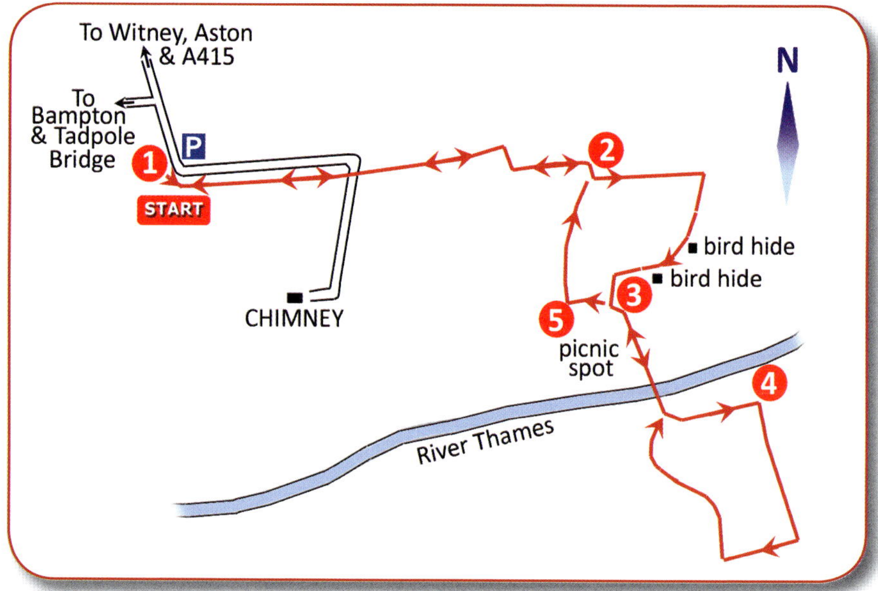

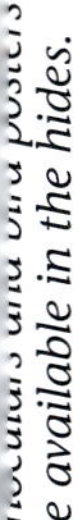
Binoculars and bird posters are available in the hides.

crossing a short boardwalk over a ditch, into another field. Continue ahead to another boardwalk. When you come to a post, turn right, following the permissive footpath through a gate and across a field to another post. Turn right again, now following a public bridleway, heading north. Pass another post and continue along the path as it veers left to a metal gate. Follow the path back to the wooden gate you passed earlier and cross the footbridge back over the Thames. Retrace your steps along the surfaced bridleway, passing the picnic tables, then continue on this path heading west until you come to a cattle grid.

5 Go through the gate beside the cattle grid then turn right and follow a permissive footpath, heading north, across the meadow until you come to a gate. Go through the gate and turn left to retrace your steps round the edge of the field to the metal gate. Walk across the field ahead of you to another metal gate, cross the road and follow the footpath back to the car park.

◆ Background Notes ◆

The **Berkshire, Buckinghamshire and Oxfordshire Wildlife Trust** owns and manages the Chimney Meadows site. It is their largest nature reserve and is a nationally important neutral grassland area. The fields were once arable but are now being turned into grasslands filled with a variety of grasses and flowers, providing a haven for insects and small mammals, as well as ground-nesting lapwings, skylarks and curlews. The wet meadows flood in winter, providing the perfect habitat for wading birds and overwintering wildfowl. Ongoing conservation work to maintain this landscape is carried out by the Friends of Chimney Meadows Volunteer Group. If you would like to be involved, contact the BBOWT Office, (01367 870904), or write to Chimney Meadows Nature Reserve, Chimney, Bampton, Oxon OX18 2EH.

Witney Lake and Meadows

Exploring a Cotswold Town and a Valley

In the watermeadows.

The historic market town of Witney is the largest town in the Oxfordshire Cotswolds. Since medieval times, it has been known for its wool, and the money brought to the town from the wool trade is reflected in the architecture of its buildings. This walk starts by the 17th-century Buttercross, where farmers' wives once came to sell their butter and eggs, before heading for Witney Lake and the water meadows by the River Windrush. The end of the walk passes the archaeological remains of the 12th-century Bishop's Palace and 13th-century St Mary's church.

Getting there Witney is 10 miles west of Oxford, with the A40 passing through the southern tip of the town. As you drive into Witney, follow the council signs for parking which will direct you to the available spaces. There is a regular Stagecoach bus service to Witney from Oxford.

Length of walk 3 miles
Time 2 hours
Terrain Pavements, surfaced paths and fields. The walk passes through meadows where cattle graze. There are no stiles and the walk is suitable for buggies.
Start/Parking There are two free town centre car parks, Marriotts Walk multi-storey car park off Woodford Way and Woolgate Centre. They are both within easy walking distance of the Buttercross, which is at the western end of the High Street, on the corner of Church Green (GR SP 356097).
Map Explorer Map 180 Oxford
Refreshments There are tables and benches by the side of Witney Lake for picnics. Alternatively, visit one of the many pubs, restaurants or tea shops in Witney.

The Walk

1 From the Buttercross, go over the road with care and walk down Corn Street. Opposite

Feeding the ducks at Witney Lake.

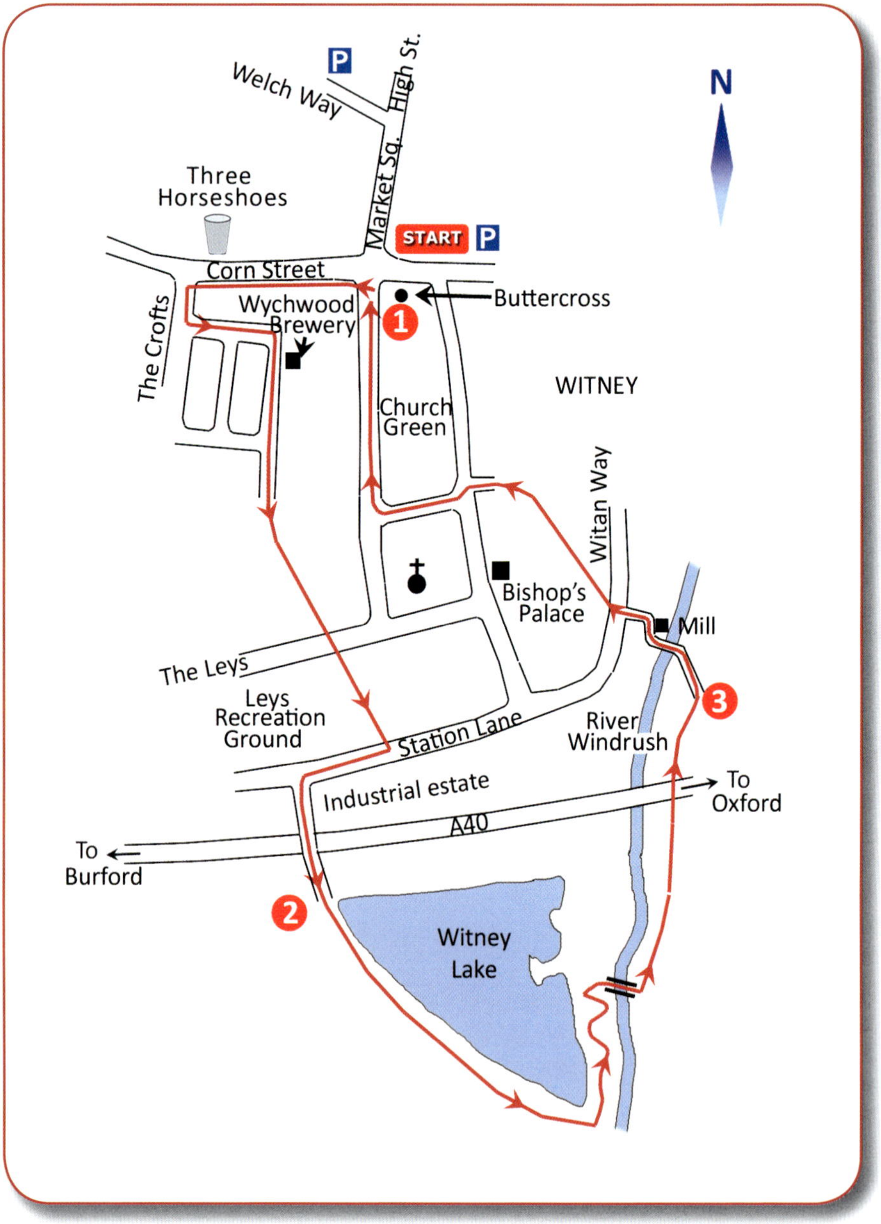

Kiddiwalks in Oxfordshire

◆ Fun Things to See and Do ◆

At the start of the walk, younger children will enjoy stopping for a play in **Leys play area** at the recreation ground. At Witney Lake there are always plenty of **ducks to watch and feed**.

Older children could find out more about the history of Witney in the beautiful stone buildings of **Cogges Manor Farm**. This working museum has a mud pie kitchen and story sty, as well as ex-battery rescue chickens. Its aim is to show children what Oxfordshire rural life was like on a Victorian farm. The museum closes in the winter, but for information on special events in the winter and opening times, visit their website at www.cogges.org.uk.

the Three Horseshoes pub, take the left turn into The Crofts. Almost immediately turn left again, passing the beer garden for the Chequers Inn and then Wychwood Brewery. The road narrows to a lane, but continue ahead, down an alleyway with some Cotswold stone houses on your right and a green on your left. Follow the footpath by the right of Leys Recreation Ground, passing a toilet block, then tennis courts, a skate park and children's play area. Come out of the park and turn right along a busy road and walk to the traffic lights. Cross the road and turn left down Station Lane. Walk through a small industrial estate and then a subway that takes you under the A40. Ignore the footbridge on your right and walk through the gate ahead of you into Witney Lake and Meadows Country Park.

2 Follow the path ahead, with the lake on your left and Emma's Dike on your right. Walk round the southern tip of the lake. As you walk along the eastern edge of the lake, with the River Windrush on your right, look out for a concrete footbridge. Leave the lake behind you and cross the footbridge, turning left to walk through a kissing gate into a large meadow, where there are sometimes cattle. Walk across the meadow, keeping the fence on your left to another wooden gate that you can see ahead of you. There is a yellow

arrow by the side of the gate to show you are on a public footpath. Walk ahead through some trees to a kissing gate, then through a subway that takes you back under the A40. Walk through another kissing gate before heading away from the road with the Windrush on your left, and beyond the river, the industrial estate that you walked through at the start of the route. Go through a metal kissing gate and follow the footpath across meadows and under some telegraph wires. Shortly, you will see St Mary's 150-ft spire on your left.

3 A gate takes you out of the Country Park. Walk along a lane until you come to a disused mill. Turn left and walk with the mill on your right over a footbridge. Then follow a surfaced track a short distance to the busy Witan Way. Cross the road with care and walk through the staggered metal railings in front of you and along a footpath with stone walls either side, and the church spire in front of you. The path ends at the corner of the picturesque Church Green, with the Buttercross at the northern end of the green. To explore the ruins of the Bishop's Palace, turn left and walk across the drive of Mount House to view the archaeological site. St Mary's church is also worth a visit. The north transept has a beautiful 14th-century window and you can see the brass-topped alter tomb of the wealthy wool merchant, Sir Richard Wennan, and his two wives.

◆ Background Notes ◆

Archaeological excavations in the Witney area have revealed loom weights and spindles dating back to the Iron Age. By medieval times the economy of the Cotswolds was based on cloth production and sheep farming, and the fortunes of Witney as a manufacturer and exporter of wool are shown in its **coat of arms**. The green background and blue wavy line show the green fields and fast-flowing River Windrush that surround the town, both needed for a successful wool industry. As the sheep grazed in the meadows, the water from the Windrush was used for washing, scouring and dyeing the wool, while water power drove the milling machinery. A paschal lamb sits at the top of the coat of arms while a blanket and glove show the two main products that Witney's many looms produced.

North Leigh Roman Villa

Discovering a Roman Villa by the River Evenlode

This is a lovely walk for a summer's day, as you follow the Wychwood Way across fields and through shady woods. The route passes two pretty Oxfordshire villages before following a stretch of the River Evenlode as it meanders through water meadows, leading you to the remains of a large Roman villa with an impressive mosaic floor.

Kiddiwalks in Oxfordshire

Getting there This walk starts in the village of East End. From the A44, at the roundabout south of Woodstock, take the turning for the A4095, passing through Bladon and Long Hanborough. Look out for the brown tourist sign and turn right for East End and the Roman villa, then turn right again and follow the narrow road into East End.

Length of walk 3 miles
Time 3 hours
Terrain Some stiles, steps and short uphill sections. A stretch of road with no pavement. Not suitable for buggies.
Start/Parking Park safely on the verge in East End. There is a small lay-by opposite the post box by Boddington House, which is near the start of the walk. There are lots of footpaths leaving the main road in East End. This walk follows the Wychwood Way, and the footpath sign is just south of the phone box (GR SP400144).
Map OS Explorer 180 Oxford
Refreshments In the middle of the walk you could make a small diversion to the Cock Inn at Combe (☎ 01993 891288) by continuing along the road, rather than turning left by the school. It is open every day for lunches, except Mondays, and has a beer garden and covered patio area. Alternatively, the bank by the side of the Roman villa is an ideal picnic spot.

The Walk

1 Follow the footpath sign for the Wychwood Way signed 'Bridleway Hanborough 1' along the side of a large field, with a hedgerow on your right. When you pass some newly planted trees fenced off with wooden posts, look out for your turning on the left. Ignore the first path

◆ Fun Things to See and Do ◆

Children can **paddle** in the shallow waters of the Evenlode. There are **sheep, cows, horses and rabbits** in the fields they walk through. Older children will enjoy the **history** of the Roman villa at the end of the walk.

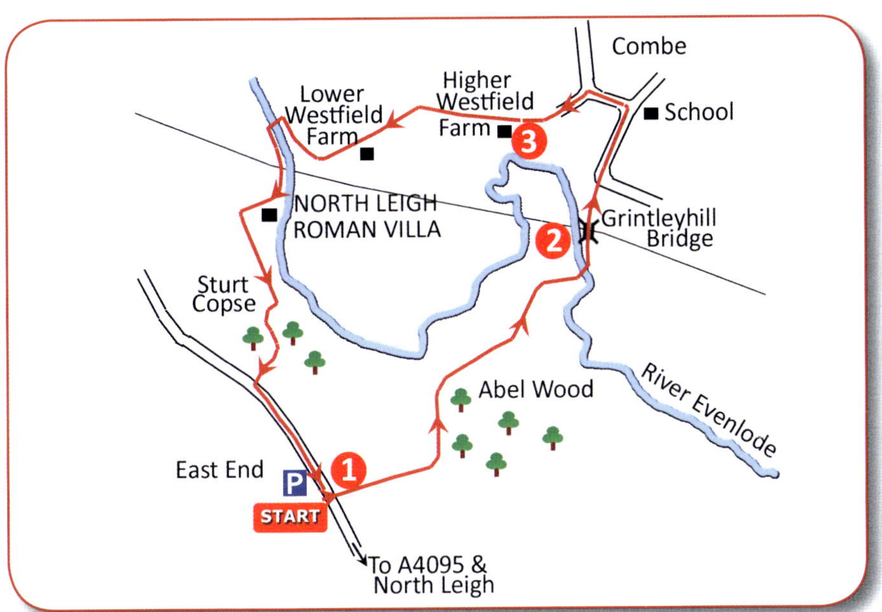

on the left, but shortly afterwards there is a junction of paths and a wooden post. Turn left here, to follow the Wychwood Way by the edge of Abel Wood. Follow the path, keeping the stream on your left, to cross a small footbridge and continue a short distance to another larger footbridge which takes you over a stile and into a field. Walk across the field to reach the banks of the River Evenlode, then turn left and follow the path by the side of the river until you come to another stile and footbridge. The bridge on your left is Grintleyhill bridge, which you will soon cross, but first go over another smaller footbridge and follow the footpath sign, veering left up some steps. The path winds uphill past blackberry bushes to meet a rutted path. Turn left, still following the Wychwood Way with a wire fence on your right and beautiful views over the valley beyond.

2 Go through a gate and now cross Grintleyhill bridge, which takes you over the railway. Follow the path until you meet a road by the edge of the village of Combe. Turn left and walk with care by the side of the road until you come to a primary school. Turn

Kiddiwalks in Oxfordshire

left opposite the school down West End. Follow this road, turning left again, to the end of West End, passing Chatterpie Lane on your right and continue ahead passing a sign for a cul-de-sac on your left.

3 Pass Higher Westfield Farm and continue downhill on this path as it becomes a paved farm track. The path veers left by a Thames Water plant then passes Lower Westfield Farm. Just after the farm, go through a kissing gate on your left and follow the footpath down the field. Head right at the bottom of the field, cross a stile, then cross the footbridge over the River Evenlode. Turn left and follow the path with the river on your left. Go under a railway bridge and cross another stile. Cross the field

to the kissing gate, then follow the side of the field for about 200 yards until you come to a gap in the hedge which leads you to the remains of the Roman villa. When you have finished exploring the site, pass the mosaic shelter on your right and go through the gate which is also on your right. Walk across the field to a kissing gate which leads into Sturt Copse. Turn right and follow the footpath along a winding woodland path that leads uphill. You pass the occasional post which shows you are on the right path. A gate leads you to the road into East End, with a green sign next to it saying that you have walked 1½ miles from Combe. Turn left here and walk along the grass verge back through the village of East End to your car.

◆ Background Notes ◆

The **Roman villa** is owned by English Heritage, it is free to visit and open all year. There is an information board which explains the site and shows a floor plan of the villa in the 4th century AD. It was abandoned in the 5th century, when the Romans left Britain.

The 3rd-century **mosaic floor** was excavated between 1812 and 1814, then lifted and relaid in 1929. It is housed in a stone hut to protect it from the weather and souvenir hunters, who destroyed two other mosaics on this site. There is a large viewing window and you can clearly see the design of the mosaic, featuring the heads of birds, geometric patterns and a guilloche twisted rope design.

Blenheim Park

Landscaped Parkland by a Baroque Palace

Blenheim Palace is the birthplace of Sir Winston Churchill and has been a World Heritage Site since 1987. Its grounds are vast, covering 2,100 acres to the west of Woodstock. Although you have to pay to enter the Palace and formal gardens, there are public footpaths and bridleways criss-crossing the estate, allowing free access to the landscaped park, designed by Lancelot 'Capability' Brown in the 1760s for the 4th Earl of Marlborough. There are splendid views of Blenheim Palace, the Column of Victory, the Lake and the Grand Bridge. This walk starts in the delightful town of Woodstock and takes you through a gate into Blenheim Estate to follow a shady woodland path by the edge of the picturesque lake. You can then either continue the walk via a section of the Wychwood Way and the Great Park, or return to the Grand Bridge to visit Blenheim Palace and the formal gardens.

Getting there Woodstock is 8 miles north of Oxford on the A44. There is a regular Stagecoach bus service to the town from Oxford.

Length of walk 2½ or 3¼ miles
Time 2 or 3 hours
Terrain Level walking along surfaced paths and sheep-grazed grassland. Sheep, pheasants and a stile make it unsuitable for dogs.
Start/Parking There is a long-stay car park on Hensington Road in Woodstock, or find a spot on one of the residential roads where there are no parking restrictions. From Park Street in the centre of Woodstock, pass the Oxfordshire Museum on your right and turn down Chaucer Lane. At the bottom of the lane, go down the 40 steps of Hosgrove Hill then turn left by the busy A44 for a short distance. Just after the zebra crossing and before the Black Prince pub, there are two large green gates with the number 95 on them (GR SP443169).
Map OS Explorer 180 Oxford
Refreshments In Woodstock, the Star Inn (☎ 01993 811373) has a children's menu and welcomes families while the Oxfordshire Museum has a café by the dinosaur garden and is free to enter. Blenheim Palace has several restaurants.

The Walk

1 Go through the large green gates with the number 95 on them, then through the gate to Blenheim Park which is in front of you on the left, noting the rules on the gate. Turn right and follow the surfaced path. When you come to Fisheries Cottage, turn left and cut across the grass in

◆ Fun Things to See and Do ◆

Blenheim Palace has compiled **13 trails and activity sheets** for children that can be downloaded from their website (http://www.blenheimpalace.com/education/ Trails-and-Activity-sheets.html). These sheets range from a Tree Trail for younger children to National Curriculum-linked maths and geography trails for older children, with some to be completed in the park and others in the formal gardens.

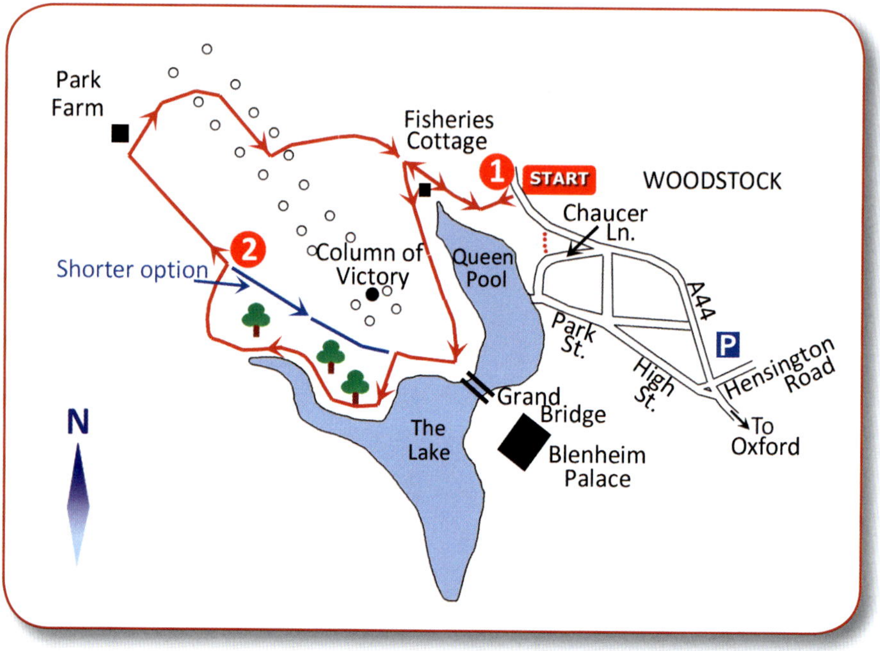

front of the cottage to the surfaced path. Now turn left and head south along this path with Queen Pool on your left. As you reach the end of this path, you suddenly see the magnificent Blenheim Palace directly in front of you across the Grand Bridge. The path ends at a grassy triangle in front of the bridge. Don't cross the bridge, instead turn right, following the path back the way you came but on the other side of the grass, with the Column of Victory ahead on your right. Look out for a gate, about 50 yards along the path on

your left. Go through the gate and walk towards the trees to the lake, created by 'Capability' Brown from the River Glyme. Follow this shady path by the western tip of the lake for nearly one mile. Ignore a grassy path leading off to your right and continue ahead, leaving the lake behind you and with a wooden fence on your left and raised ground on your right. Stay on this path for a short distance until you meet a surfaced path. Turn right and follow this path gently uphill to a triangle of grass with a 'caution pheasants on road' sign and another path in front of you, heading to the left and right. Now you have a choice, turn right to return to the Grand Bridge and Blenheim Palace, or turn left for the longer walk.

2 To complete the longer route, follow the surfaced path to Park Farm, this is a good spot for collecting conkers in autumn. The path leads you to the right, in front of the farm buildings, to cross a cattle grid into a large field. Walk across this field to a stile, keeping the fence on your right. Cross the stile and walk towards an avenue of trees. Turn right and walk along the Grand Avenue towards the Column of Victory ahead. Cross a cattle grid and continue along the path, until you see Fisheries Cottage, which you passed at the start of the walk. Take the path on the left and continue for a short distance until you see the green gates on your left.

◆ Background Notes ◆

The land and money to build **Blenheim Palace** were a gift from Queen Anne to the soldier and diplomat **John Churchill, 1st Duke of Marlborough** after his victory against the French during the Wars of the Spanish Succession. Churchill had a brilliant military career. His finest moment was as the victorious military commander at the Battle of Blenheim, in August 1704.

But this wasn't to be the only battle that the Palace would be associated with. Churchill's wife, **Sarah, 1st Duchess of Marlborough**, fell out spectacularly with the architect, Sir John Vanbrugh, over the cost and design of the house, causing him to leave the project. She then, even more disastrously, fell out with Queen Anne, despite having been her friend and confidante since before she was Queen. The Marlboroughs were forced to leave the country, the money for the building was stopped and they did not return until after Queen Anne's death in 1714. Eventually, the Duke had to pay for the completion of the Palace himself, this time with a different architect, Vanbrugh's assistant, Hawksmoor.

Spiceball Country Park

A Fun-packed Day

There is a lot to see and do on this walk. It starts in Spiceball Country Park, Banbury's largest park, which is fringed by the River Cherwell on one side and the Oxford Canal on the other. The southern end of the park has a children's play area and a short diversion takes you to Banbury Museum and Tooley's Boatyard. You then head north along an idyllic stretch of the Oxford Canal, with ducks to feed and colourful narrowboats to spot. The route passes the edge of Grimsbury Woodland Nature Reserve, which has a signed circular walk if you want to explore. You then return to the Country Park by the side of Grimsbury reservoir, where over 100 different species of water bird have been recorded.

Getting there From junction 11 of the M40, take the A422 into Banbury. At the second roundabout take the third turning, marked with a brown tourist sign for the sailing club and Spiceball Park. Turn left, signed Thames Water, down a narrow lane. The free council car park is at the bottom of this road.

Length of walk 2½ miles
Time 2 hours
Terrain Level walk along surfaced footpaths, towpath and grass. Suitable for all-terrain pushchairs. There are six shallow steps up to the reservoir.
Start/Parking Spiceball Country Park car park. Follow the path out of the car park into Spiceball Park to start the walk (GR SP459418).
Map OS Explorer 191 Banbury, Bicester & Chipping Norton
Refreshments There is a picnic area in Spiceball Park and a family-friendly café in Banbury Museum.

The Walk

1 From the car park, take the path on your right, passing a large Grimsbury Reservoir Park Guide sign. The path veers to the right under a large road bridge, it is divided into a footpath and cycle path and leads you into Spiceball Park. Turn left at the

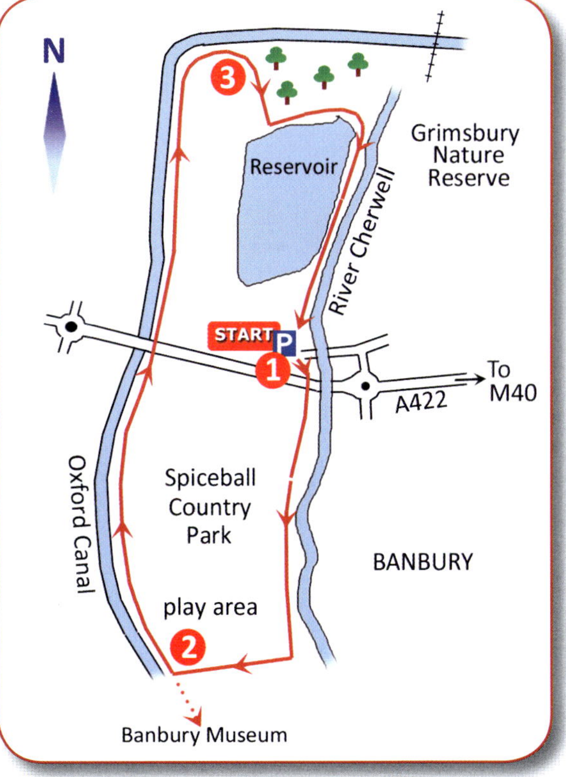

Kiddiwalks in Oxfordshire

park entrance and follow the path, keeping the Cherwell on your left. This pretty stretch of the river is dotted with lily pads and lots of wildlife for children to spot. When you come to a weir, you will see a car park ahead of you. Just before the car park, turn right and walk towards the Spiceball play area, passing some picnic tables.

2 Walk past the play area to the towpath. On your left is Tom Rolt Bridge and Castle Quay shopping centre. The museum and boatyard are just past the shopping centre. However, to continue the walk, turn right and follow the towpath under a road bridge. As you head north, the canal becomes quieter and the towpath gets narrower. When you see a metal railway

A peaceful stretch of the Oxford Canal.

bridge ahead of you, look out for a turning on the right. There are six wooden steps that lead up to a narrow path, passing a sign for Grimsbury Reservoir Nature

◆ Fun Things to See and Do ◆

This walk passes **Spiceball play area**, which is the perfect spot for children to have some fun, with picnic tables next to it for the grown-ups to have a rest and a snack. There are also two skateboard ramps in the park for older children. Some of the wooden **narrowboats** on the Oxford Canal have pots of flowers, herbs and strawberries on top. Children could read the names of the boats and pick their favourite one. There are also **ducks to feed** on the canal.

Reserve on your left. There is also a map showing the footpaths through the wood, if you want to add a detour to explore.

3 Follow the path to the reservoir, then turn left to walk round the end of the reservoir. Follow the Banbury Fringe Walk south, along a raised path, with the reservoir fenced off on your right and the River Cherwell on your left. Look out for a sign on your right describing the different birdlife on the reservoir. At the southern edge of the water, stay left on the Banbury Fringe Walk, keeping the river on your left, and go over a small weir. Go through the gate by the side of a large metal gate which leads you to the road and back to the car park.

◆ Background Notes ◆

Near the walk, **Banbury Museum** prides itself on its family-friendly approach, with a regular programme of temporary exhibitions and events. There is a café with baby changing facilities and a gift shop. It is free to enter and is open every day except Sundays. For more information about the museum, call ☎ 01295 753752 or check their website: www.banburymuseum.org

Tooley's Boatyard, also close to the route, is the oldest working dry dock in Britain. It was established in 1790 to build and repair the horse-drawn narrowboats on the canal. To arrange a one-hour guided tour of the historic boatyard, you need to pre-book by calling ☎ 01295 272917.

Two miles west of Banbury is the magnificent **Broughton Castle**. The castle was built in 1300 and enlarged in 1550. It is a classic, fairytale castle with crenellated walls, arrowslit windows and a large moat, all of which have contributed to its impressive film career. The castle has appeared in *The Madness of King George*, *Shakespeare in Love*, *Three Men and a Little Lady* and the Cinderella story of *The Slipper and the Rose*. Check prices and opening times before you visit by calling 01295 276070 or look at their website: www.broughtoncastle.com

Tusmore Park

Avenues of Trees and Parkland

Lime Avenue leads you across the parkland.

This walk starts in the sleepy village of Hardwick, which in Anglo-Saxon means a 'dwelling place for sheep'. The walk then takes you across fields and through avenues of first yew, then lime trees, to the parkland of the Tusmore estate, where indeed sheep do dwell. The private Tusmore House was built at the start of this century in the Georgian style. It is absolutely massive, and built in gleaming French limestone with a vast, pillared portico. You get the best views of the house after you have crossed the parkland, from where you can decide for yourself whether it is worth its £30 million price tag.

Getting there Hardwick is about 4 miles north of Bicester. From junction 10 of the M40, head north on the A43 towards Brackley. Turn right at the roundabout in Baynard's Green, then take the first left and stay on this road, continuing ahead at the crossroads, to follow the signs for Hardwick.

Length of walk 2¼ miles
Time 2 hours
Terrain Level walking along footpaths and across fields. Suitable for buggies.
Start/Parking Hethe Road runs through the hamlet of Hardwick. Look out for a parking space on the verge on your left. The walk starts at the bridleway which is almost opposite Roots of Hardwick farm shop (GR SP577297).
Map OS Explorer 191 Banbury, Bicester & Chipping Norton
Refreshments The Roots of Hardwick farm shop is open seven days a week. It sells ice creams and all the ingredients for a delicious picnic. The bank below the walls of Tusmore Park is a good picnic spot.

◆ Fun Things to See and Do ◆

There are lots of **pheasants** in the woodland on this walk. You can see the feeders for them dotted along the edges of the fields and woods. The male pheasants have a dark green head and neck and a red face, while the females are a more subdued mottled brown colour. They were introduced to this country by the Romans as a game bird.

Children can see how many different **nuts, seeds and leaves** they can collect on the walk, and when they get home try to identify which trees they come from. However, remind children never to pick yew berries as they are poisonous. You could also point out the difference between the evergreen and deciduous trees. Younger children will enjoy playing **hide and seek** in the woods and running between the trees in the avenue.

Kiddiwalks in Oxfordshire

11

1 Take the bridleway path signed 'Tusmore Park 1 mile' across a garden to a gate, then follow the path ahead across a large arable field. When you reach the edge of Tusmore Wood, continue ahead onto Yew Avenue, where under the large evergreen trees, the path is fringed with blackberry bushes. Come out of the woods into an area of open parkland and walk along the majestic Lime Avenue. In autumn the colours are spectacular. At the end of the trees, turn left and go through a gate to a surfaced road.

2 Turn right and walk past the walls of Tusmore House. Just after you pass the gold and black iron gates, look out for a wooden gate on your right which leads you directly across Tusmore Park. There are normally sheep here so dogs need to be on a lead. Walk across Tusmore Park to a gate on the opposite side which leads you into Park Plantation. Follow the wide gravel path ahead. When you come to a post, follow the path right, by the blue arrow. There is an impressive view of the east elevation of Tusmore House across the parkland to your right. The 32,000 cubic feet of stone for the house was quarried in Dijon,

Sheep grazing at Tusmore Park

France, and shipped in block form to Oxfordshire.

3 The path ends in a fork. Take the bridleway path on the left with a pale blue arrow, ignoring the smaller path just before it on your left. Continue along this path with Tusmore Wood on your right and a hedge on your left. The path ends at a T-junction with a post in front of you. Turn left, following the blue arrow, across the side of a field until you come to another crossroads of paths, and a blue arrow post. Take the path on your right, past a yellow arrow post, to walk for about 50 yards by the side of an arable field along a wide grassy verge. Look out for the footpath on your left; this leads you diagonally across the field, through a gap in the hedge and a line of silver birch, to cross another field, heading south. Shortly you will see the roofs of the village ahead. Follow the public footpath down a narrow path to Hethe Road and your car.

◆ Background Notes ◆

Tusmore House is the fourth house to be built on this site. First there was a small manor house, recorded in the Domesday Book of 1086. This was replaced in the second half of the 18th century with a large Classical style house and was the seat of the Earls of Effingham until 1927. It then changed hands a few times, with some alterations made, until 1960, when it was pulled down and replaced with a much smaller country house. In 2000, Wafic Saïd bought the 3,000 acre estate. He held a competition to design a replacement for the house, which was considered too small for its grand setting. One of the designs put forward was an exact replica of the original 18th-century house. The Classical-style house you see today was designed by Sir William Whitfield and won the 2004 Georgian Group prize for the 'best modern house in the classical tradition'. Wafic Saïd is one of Britain's richest men, with an estimated fortune of £1 billion. In 1996, he founded the Saïd Business School, which is part of the University of Oxford, with a £20 million donation, and he is still a benefactor of the school.

Otmoor Nature Reserve

Be a Bird Detective

Otmoor is a magical wetland landscape, with flood fields fringed with reed beds, providing the perfect habitat for water birds. The Royal Society for the Protection of Birds has made a path across the reserve which makes this an excellent walk for families with buggies. The walk is not circular, as there is no access to parts of the nature reserve due to ongoing conservation work, but you pass a bird hide and two large viewing screens, which give children a wonderful opportunity to sit and watch nature close up. As well as a wide variety of birds, this rare landscape is also home to hares, otters and butterflies. The reserve is open every day and is free to visit.

Getting there Otmoor is about 5 miles north-east of Oxford. From junction 8A of the M40, follow the A40 to the Headington roundabout on the edge of Oxford. Take the Barton exit and follow the signs to the village of Beckley. In Beckley, turn right onto the High Street and just after the Abingdon Arms pub, take a sharp left turn onto Otmoor Lane. Follow this narrow road for a mile, passing a turning to Lower Farm, until you come to the RSPB car park on your left.

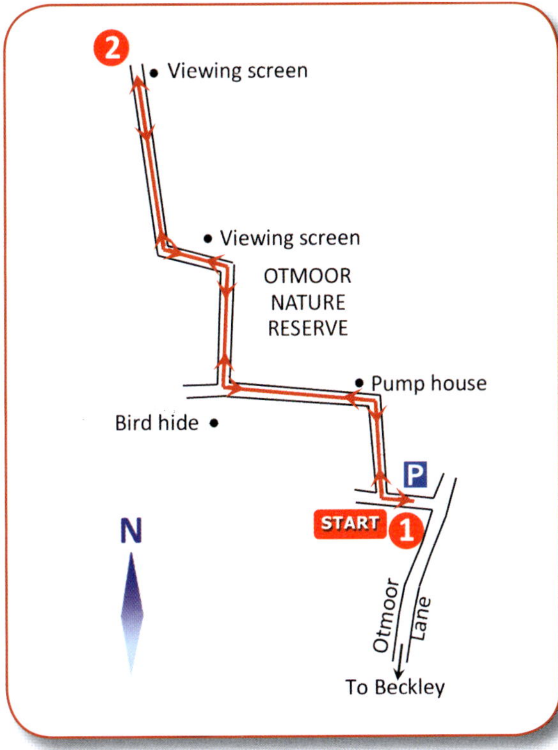

a surfaced path. Suitable for buggies. No dogs allowed in the RSPB reserve.

Start/Parking Free parking at the RSPB car park on Otmoor Lane, where the walk starts (GR SP570126).

Map OS Explorer 180 Oxford, Witney and Woodstock

Refreshments The historic Abingdon Arms in Beckley serves food every day and has an attractive beer garden (☎ 01865 351311). Alternatively, there are benches in the nature reserve for picnics.

Length of walk 3½ miles
Time 2 hours
Terrain Level walking along

❶ Walk out of the car park, turn right and go through the wooden kissing gate into the nature

◆ Fun Things to See and Do ◆

Pack your binoculars as there are always plenty of **birds to spot** on Otmoor. The path has deliberately been made below the bank so you can sneak up to the screens without the birds spotting you and flying off or hiding in the reeds. You need to sit as quietly as possible to be a **bird detective**. A bird book will help you identify the birds, otherwise bring a camera, or a pen and paper to record the different types of birds, noting their size, colour and shape. When you get home, look on the RSPB website, which has a very clear identification section (www.rspb.org.uk/wildlife/birdidentifier). There is also a children's section with fun activities and facts about birds (www.rspb.org.uk/youth).

reserve. After about 20 yards, turn right again, following the RSPB arrow on a small post. At the end of this path there is a small bench and a bird feeding station. Cross the footbridge and turn left by the pump house. Follow the path ahead, with views across the reed beds to the steeple of Charlton-on-Otmoor church. Shortly you will also see the steeple of Oddington's church in front of you. When you come to a Wetlands Watch bird hide on your left, go through the gate on your right and follow the signed visitor trail through the reserve. The path turns to the left and passes a large birdwatching screen. Looking through the screen you have an amazing view across the reed beds of the flocks of water birds. Then continue along the path to the next screen.

2 You can't go any further as beyond this point is a sensitive conservation area. Turn back to retrace your steps, passing the viewing screen and walk back to the gate. Then turn left and walk to the pump house, cross over the footbridge and head back to the car park.

Reedbeds are an important habitat for waterbirds.

◆ Background Notes ◆

The **marshland** at Otmoor was drained and fenced in the mid 19th century, following the Enclosure Acts. The fencing gave the area an artificial grid pattern that inspired **Lewis Carroll** to write of a chess-board landscape in the children's classic *Alice's Adventures in Wonderland*. The local agricultural labourers sabotaged the early attempts to build fences and dam the River Ray, as they tried to save the marshland, which they had used for breeding ducks and geese. In 1830, about 1,000 people marched around Otmoor destroying every fence they came to. The Oxfordshire Militia and Yeomanry Cavalry were called out, but the people would not disperse. They were read the Riot Act and 44 Otmoor rioters were taken to Oxford gaol. On the same day St Giles' Fair was being held in Oxford. When the locals found out what was happening, they turned on the yeoman, throwing sticks and stones, and the prisoners escaped. In the 1970s, there was another attempt to drain the area when an electrical pumping station was installed. In the 1980s, the government considered building the M40 across Otmoor. Friends of the Earth led a campaign against this and the route of the motorway was diverted east. Since 1997, a large part of Otmoor has been an RSPB nature reserve, while the pump is used to put water back into the marshland, restoring the wetlands and reedbeds.

In **spring**, you can spot curlews and snipe, who both have long thin beaks, as well as broods of fluffy ducklings. Lapwings, tufted ducks and redshanks all breed here. Lapwings are very protective of their nests and will chase off any other birds who get too close to their chicks. Skylarks fly over the grassland, and their song is unmistakable. In **summer**, the meadows and hedgerows attract butterflies, while dragonflies dart over the water. Look out for hobbies soaring in the sky. These small birds of prey have long, narrow wings and are a type of falcon. They hunt small birds and insects with their long talons, then transfer the food to their beak mid-flight. **Autumn** brings flocks of migrating wading birds, including common sandpipers and little egrets. **In winter**, the flood fields are a haven for thousands of overwintering water birds.

Hampton Poyle and Thrupp Wide

A Crash, a Curse and a Ruin

This walk crosses classic Oxfordshire countryside to the River Cherwell, passing the deserted village of Hampton Gay. Here you can see the picturesque Elizabethan ruins of a manor house, destroyed by fire in 1887, supposedly as the result of a curse for refusing to help the victims of a nearby train crash. The walk then follows the banks of Thrupp Wide, an idyllic stretch of the Oxford Canal, before passing through the edge of woodland and across meadows to return to Hampton Poyle.

13

Getting there From the southern edge of Kidlington, head north along Bicester Road. Turn left onto Oxford Road and drive through Hampton Poyle, past the Bell pub, and straight on down Church Lane to the church.

Length of Walk 3½ miles
Time 3 hours
Terrain Flat field paths and towpath. There are lots of stiles on this walk and some of the fields you walk through have sheep and horses in them. The walk is not suitable for buggies or dogs.
Start/Parking There is a grass verge in front of the church at Hampton Poyle where the walk starts. Be careful not to block access to Manor Farm gates (GR SP498155).

Map OS Explorer 180 Oxford, Witney & Woodstock
Refreshments Thrupp Wide has picnic tables and benches by the swing bridge overlooking the canal. Annie's Tea Room in Canal Yard, Thrupp, is open every day and serves sandwiches, soup, cakes and ice cream.

The Walk

1 This walk starts by following the Oxford Greenbelt Way. With the 13th-century church of St Mary the Virgin on your left, cross the stile into a field. Cross this field heading right to two more stiles, then about 20 yards ahead on your left there are two more stiles that lead you into another large field. Veer right to cross a stile in the corner, then cross the next field, over the stile and across a small footbridge. Bear right over

◆ Fun Things to See and Do ◆

At Thrupp Canoe and Kayak Hire Centre, opposite Annie's Tea Room in Thrupp yard, you can **hire a canoe or a kayak** for an hour, half a day or a full day to explore the Oxford Canal and River Cherwell. For prices and more information, call ☎ 01865 842708 or look online at www. tckh.co.uk. For younger children, there are **plenty of ducks** on the canal who are always eager to share your picnic, as well as colourful narrowboats to spot. You also pass lots of **sheep and horses** in the fields.

the next field to cross two small footbridges through some trees. Go directly ahead and over another stile. You can now see the small church of St Giles at Hampton Gay ahead of you, built in the 1760s

Feeding the ducks on the Oxford Canal.

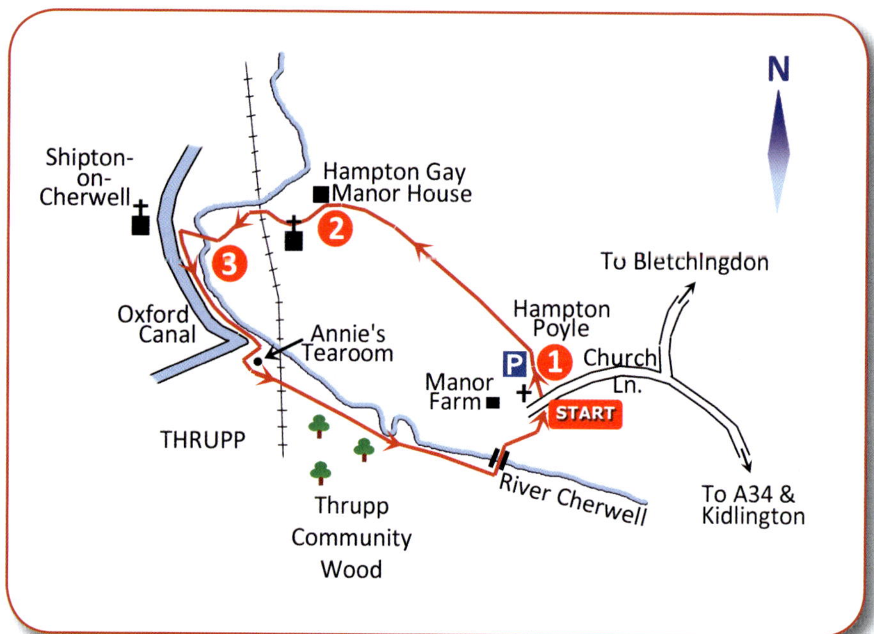

on the foundations of an earlier church. Walk left round the edge of the field towards another stile, then head towards the church. You come to a kissing gate with St Giles on your left and the eerie ruins of the 16th-century gothic Manor House on your right. Stay on the footpath as the ruins are in a dangerous state of decay.

2 Continue ahead past hawthorn bushes towards the sound of the weir on the River Cherwell. Then bear left across the field to a kissing gate and walk across a metal walkway by the river, which takes you under the railway. Go through a kissing gate and walk diagonally across the next field and past a line of telegraph poles. Cross the River Cherwell over a small suspension bridge. Go straight ahead through the next field to cross a stile by the side of a metal farm gate.

3 Don't cross the bridge, instead turn left to follow the Oxford Canal, with the church of the Holy Cross at Shipton-on-Cherwell on the other side of the water. When you come to Thrupp, don't cross the swing bridge, instead

Hampton Poyle and Thrupp Wide

turn left and walk through Canal Yard, passing some cottages to walk ahead along a farm track, under the railway and through a gate. Follow the path keeping the Cherwell on your left, as it meanders through the Thrupp Community Woodland. Eventually, you come out of the woods to a large field with a church steeple ahead of you. Follow the left edge of the field, with the Cherwell still on your left, until you come to a concrete footbridge. Cross 'White Bridge' then go over a stile and continue ahead to a small footbridge with a metal gate either side. Go straight across the field to another stile. You can see the farm buildings of Manor Farm ahead of you now. Walk across the field and over a stile to the road and your car.

◆ Background Notes ◆

The walk takes you under the railway near **Hampton Gay** which was the scene of a terrible train crash one snowy Christmas Eve in 1874. A Great Western train from Paddington to Birmingham was packed with passengers travelling home for Christmas. Near Hampton Gay, the carriages derailed and crashed over the bridge into the frozen waters of the Oxford Canal. Thirty-four people died and nearly 100 were injured. Lord Randolph Churchill came from Woodstock with a party to offer help and the injured were taken to Radcliffe Infirmary. There are stories that Hampton Gay Manor House refused to offer shelter to the injured passengers, thus putting a curse on the house which was gutted by fire 13 years later. The manor house has been a ruin ever since and is on the Historic Oxfordshire Buildings 'at risk' register. The present owner has submitted plans to build a 21st-century home within the original walls, propping up the stone walls from behind with the concrete walls of the new house, and generating electricity from the river.

Part of the appeal of the popular television series *Morse*, are the evocative settings, as the series was filmed in Oxford and the surrounding countryside. Morse was keen on drinking in Oxfordshire's beautiful old pubs. The Boat Inn and this stretch of the Oxford Canal featured in the episode called *The Last Enemy*.

Christ Church Meadow and Oxford's Dreaming Spires

The Isis, Gargoyles and Grotesques

Oxford's history stretches back to the 9th century, when it was founded by Alfred the Great, as he created a network of fortified towns across his kingdom. Oxford is a fascinating city for children to explore. This walk takes you through the peaceful Christ Church Meadow to the River Thames. This stretch of the Thames, within the city boundaries of Oxford, is known as the Isis and it was along this stretch of the river where Lewis Carroll, a fellow of Christ Church College, first told a little girl called Alice Liddell the tale of *Alice's Adventures in Wonderland*. The walk leaves the river to explore some of Oxford's famous landmarks, with gargoyles and grotesques peering down from the rooftops for children to spot along the way.

Christ Church Meadow & Oxford's Dreaming Spires

Getting there Oxford is east of the M40, with the A34 running from north to south. The train station is within walking distance of the centre.

Length of walk 2 miles
Time 2 hours
Terrain Level walking along pavements and through the park. Suitable for buggies.
Start/Parking Use Oxford's efficient Park and Ride bus service, with 5 large car parks positioned around the ring road. The walk starts at the Carfax tower, which is at the junction of four roads: St Aldate's, Cornmarket Street, High Street and Queen Street (GR SP513062).
Map OS Explorer Map 180 Oxford
Refreshments The Head of the River on Folly Bridge, St Aldate's, is a family-friendly pub with an outside seating area looking out over the river (☎ 01865 721600). The café in Modern Art Oxford, Pembroke Street, has high chairs and baby-changing facilities.

The Walk

1 From Carfax tower, turn right and walk down busy St Aldate's, passing Christ Church College on your left. The Great Hall at Christ College was the inspiration for the Hogwarts dining hall while the staircase leading up to the

◆ Fun Things to See and Do ◆

The best way to look at Oxford is upwards. As you walk, see how many **gargoyles**, **grotesques** and other animals you can see carved into the walls or clinging to the roofs of the colleges and churches. A gargoyle is a decorative water spout, which stops the wall from getting damp, while grotesques look similar, but don't spout water. These carved heads are based on mythical creatures, demons, animals or sometimes even professors who taught at the colleges.

Younger children can **feed the ducks and geese** in Christ Church Meadow, and **spot the squirrels** scampering from tree to tree.

Kiddiwalks in Oxfordshire

hall was used in several scenes of the Harry Potter films. Almost opposite the Alice in Wonderland shop, and just before the traffic lights, turn left through Visitors' Gate, passing a sign on the right for 'Christ Church Meadow'.

Follow the Broad Walk for a short distance, passing a small war memorial garden then turn right down New Walk. When you get to the river, turn left to follow the riverbank. Ignore a footbridge on your right which leads to the

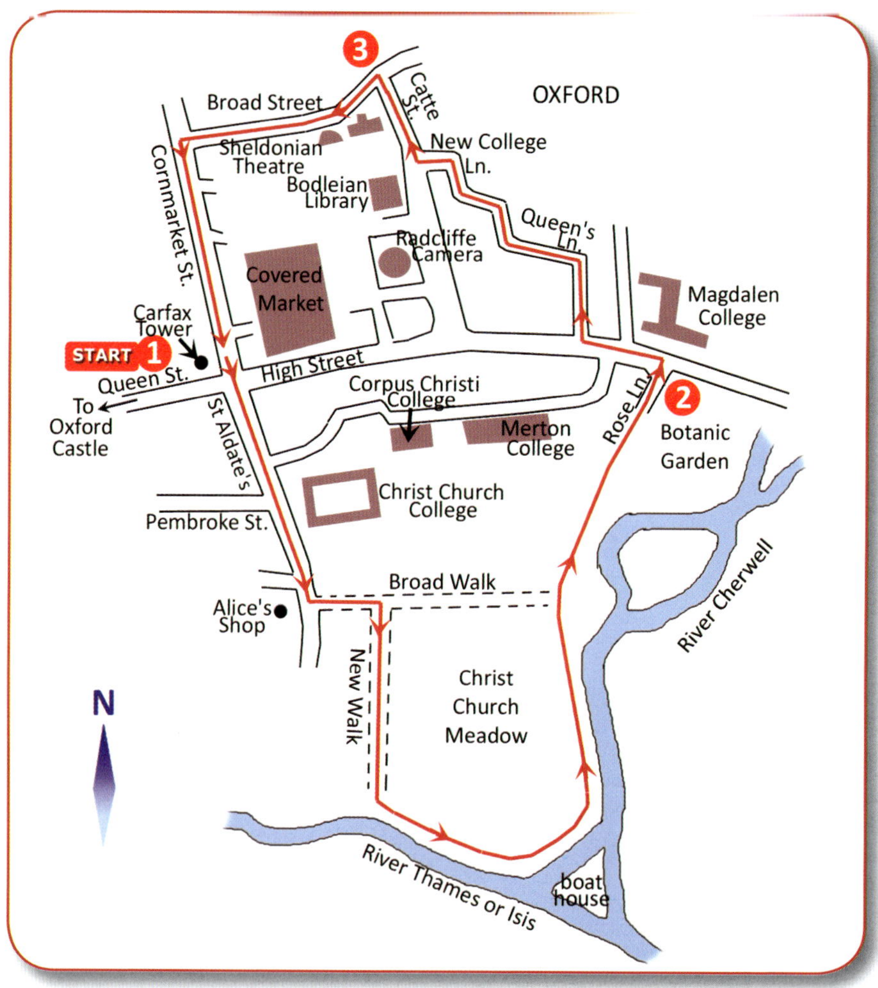

Christ Church Meadow & Oxford's Dreaming Spires

boat houses and continue ahead, now following the River Cherwell as it leads you to the edge of the Botanic Garden. Keep ahead with iron railings now on either side of the path and walk towards some imposing wrought-iron gates. If you have a buggy, you might have to fold it up to get through these gates.

2 Walk down Rose Lane. At the end of the lane, you could take a detour by visiting Magdalen College; there is a herd of deer in winter in Magdalen Grove, just north of the college. To continue the walk, turn left and walk down High Street, passing a traditional sweet shop, which your children might want to visit. Turn right down Queen's Lane, stopping to peep through the railings at the statue of Sir Edmund of Abingdon, reading in the churchyard. Follow the lane as it twists past New College on the right and Hertford College on the left. It is now New College Lane and looking up on the right you will see a row of fantastical animals and grotesques grinning down at you. Look behind you to see a winged creature on top of Queen's College library. Walk under the Bridge of Sighs and the Bodleian Library is in front of you. Look up to see the grotesques and the initials 'TB'. Thomas Bodley provided the funds for the library in 1602. The Radcliffe Camera is to the left of the library, but to continue the walk, turn right down Catte Street.

3 At the end of Catte Street, turn left onto Broad Street. Stop at the Sheldonian Theatre to spot the 'emperors' on top of the pillars and look for the nine muses on top of the Clarendon Building. Continue down Broad Street to Cornmarket Street, where you turn left. You are now in the heart of Oxford's bustling shopping area and at the end of this road is the Carfax Tower. As you walk down Cornmarket Street, it is worth taking a detour to see Oxford's famous covered market, which is a feast for the senses. To visit the market, take the left turn down the Golden Cross passageway, walk past Pizza Express and into the market.

◆ Background Notes ◆

Alice Liddell, daughter of the Dean at Christ Church College, was the inspiration for the fictional character of **Alice in Wonderland.** Charles Dodgson (1832–98), who wrote under the pseudonym Lewis Carroll, taught mathematics at Christ Church and was a friend of the Liddell family. Alice's favourite sweet shop was opposite Christ Church and is now an Alice in Wonderland themed gift shop. There are two illustrations showing the front of the shop in the original book. Dodgson used to hire rowing boats for Alice and her two sisters to take them on trips along this stretch of the river. He also took them to Oxford's Museum of Natural History to see the dinosaur skeletons and the dodo. On a rowing trip in the summer of 1862, he told a story about a little girl called Alice and a magical rabbit hole. Alice Liddell begged him to write the story down for her. *Alice's Adventures in Wonderland* was published in 1865 and *Through the Looking Glass* in 1872, with both books dedicated to Alice Liddell.

Carfax Tower is all that is left of the 13th-century St Martin's church. Traffic caused the road to be widened and the church was knocked down in 1896, leaving the tower standing alone with the Oxford motto below the clock: 'Fortis est Veritas' (Truth is Strength). You can climb the 99 narrow spiral steps to the top of the tower for an excellent view across Oxford's dreaming spires. The tower is open daily and there is an admittance charge.

Shotover Country Park

Tree Climbing and Den Building

Shotover Country Park, on the eastern edge of Oxford, was once part of the Royal Forest of Shotover and a hunting ground for noblemen. Oxford City Council have managed the site since the 1930s and have clearly labelled various walks, making it easy to explore the maze of paths without worrying about getting lost. It is a Site of Special Scientific Interest, with heathland, wetland, woods and grassland providing a haven for a wide range of wildlife. The woodland floor is carpeted with wild flowers in spring and summer, the trees are filled with the song of woodland birds, and foxes, muntjac and roe deer find cover in the bracken. Nearby is the tranquil CS Lewis Nature Reserve and children's nature trail. The pond and surrounding woodland provided C.S. Lewis with his inspiration for the landscape of Narnia. This is within walking distance of Shotover and is well worth visiting at the end of the walk, see *Background Notes* for directions.

Kiddiwalks in Oxfordshire

15

Getting there From Headington, follow Old Road east, over the A4142, then continue ahead up a steep, single-track road to the car park.

Length of walk 1½ miles
Time 1 hour
Terrain Woodland paths, with some steep sections. Suitable for all-terrain pushchairs.
Start/Parking Shotover Country Park free car park. This walk starts from the southern edge of the car park by Mary Sadler's Field and follows the yellow circle route (GR SP565063).
Map OS Explorer 180 Oxford
Refreshments There is no shortage of places to eat in Oxford, otherwise bring a picnic and find a bench or handy tree trunk along the walk.

The Walk

1 From the car park, walk past the large

sign for Shotover Country Park and into Mary Sadler's Field, a grassy open area. Turn right, passing a large noticeboard and head downhill, passing a yellow circle sign on your right, then turn left at the bottom. The path goes first down, then uphill, until you come to a T-junction where you turn right, then almost immediately right again. Continue along the path with views through the trees towards

There are plenty of trees to climb.

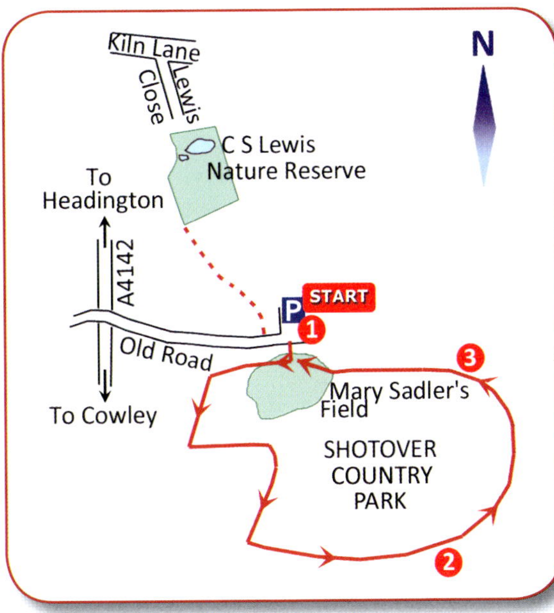

2 Continue straight on to the end of this path. Then join the surfaced track from the right which leads you straight on and slightly uphill. There is another yellow post here to show that you are heading in the right direction. When you come to a large blackberry thicket on your right, leave the track and take the steep path on your left into the woods, passing another yellow post.

Cowley. At the bottom of this path, turn left and continue through the woods. This is a good spot for den building.

3 Look out for a right turn in the woods, then follow the path as it weaves through the trees and over fallen tree trunks, following

◆ Fun Things to See and Do ◆

These ancient woods are filled with **trees to climb** and fallen branches for **den building**. In late summer, there are blackberries to pick, while in autumn, the woodland floor is carpeted with fallen leaves to kick and play in.

Older children could practise their **compass skills**. Show your child how to find north, south, east and west with a compass, then challenge them to tell you in which direction they are walking at various points of the walk.

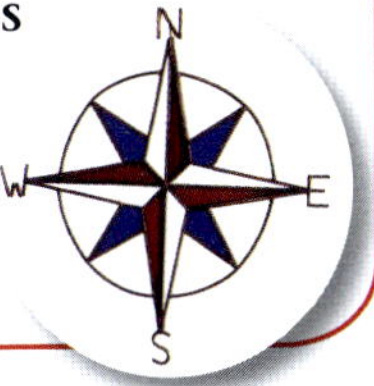

the yellow signs. Eventually, the path leads uphill to a wider track where you turn left, then after about 20 yards there is a right then left turn. Pass some open ground with a clear view to the left, then head back into the woods, crossing a track and continuing ahead past a large oak tree. There is a yellow post behind this tree and a path which leads up to the right, past broadleaf trees, until you come to a carved stone bench on your right. Walk past the bench into Mary Sadler's Field, and you will see the car park.

◆ Background Notes ◆

C.S. Lewis (1898–1963), author of the classic series of children's books, *The Chronicles of Narnia,* was a fellow of Magdalen College in Oxford, where he was an English tutor for 29 years. He lived in The Kilns from 1929 until his death in 1963. A path led from his house to the pond in the heart of the CS Lewis Nature Reserve. It was while he was living here that he wrote the Narnia series and it is easy to see how this tranquil spot provided the inspiration. Lewis also had evacuees staying at his house during the Second World War, to escape the bombing in London. Now, The Kilns is owned by the CS Lewis Foundation as a private Christian study centre, but the nature reserve is free to enter and is open all year.

The pond in the **CS Lewis Nature Reserve** is a flooded Victorian clay pit, with frogs and toads spawning in spring, while dazzling dragonflies and damselflies dance over the water in summer. A public footpath connects the nature reserve with Shotover Country Park. From the car park, walk down Old Road for a short distance, then take the footpath on your right for about ¼ mile, heading north-west through trees to enter the southern corner of the reserve, then follow the signed path. Alternatively, drive back down Old Road over the A4142 and turn right onto Quarry Road. Stay on this road and go straight on at the traffic lights onto Kiln Lane. Lewis Close is the fourth turning on the right. Park at the end of the cul-de-sac and follow the path between the houses to the reserve. There is a map and information board at the northern tip of the reserve.

Abingdon and the River Thames

Exploring Abbey Ruins

On the Thames Path.

This walk explores Andersey Island, south of Abingdon, where in summer the sky is filled with the song of skylarks. It then returns to the historic market town via a stretch of the Thames Path, crossing the river at a weir to walk by Abbey Stream. You can then walk through the historic heart of Abingdon, with a chance to explore the ruins of Abingdon Abbey.

Kiddiwalks in Oxfordshire

Getting there Abingdon is 8 miles south of Oxford. From the A34, take the A415 at the roundabout following the signs for Abingdon town centre and Abingdon Bridge. The car park is immediately south of the bridge on the A415.

Length of walk 2 miles
Time 1½ hours
Terrain Level walking along pavements and field paths. Take care with younger children crossing Abingdon weir. Suitable for all-terrain buggies.

Start/Parking Rye Farm pay and display car park (GR SU501968).
Map OS Explorer 170 Abingdon, Wantage & Vale of White Horse
Refreshments The Abbey Meadows play area is the perfect spot for a picnic. Abingdon has cafés, restaurants and pubs with beer gardens looking out over the river.

The Walk

1 Walk out of the car park and turn right along a tarmac track, passing a large sign on your right for Kingfisher Barn bed and breakfast. This track is raised above the surrounding land and

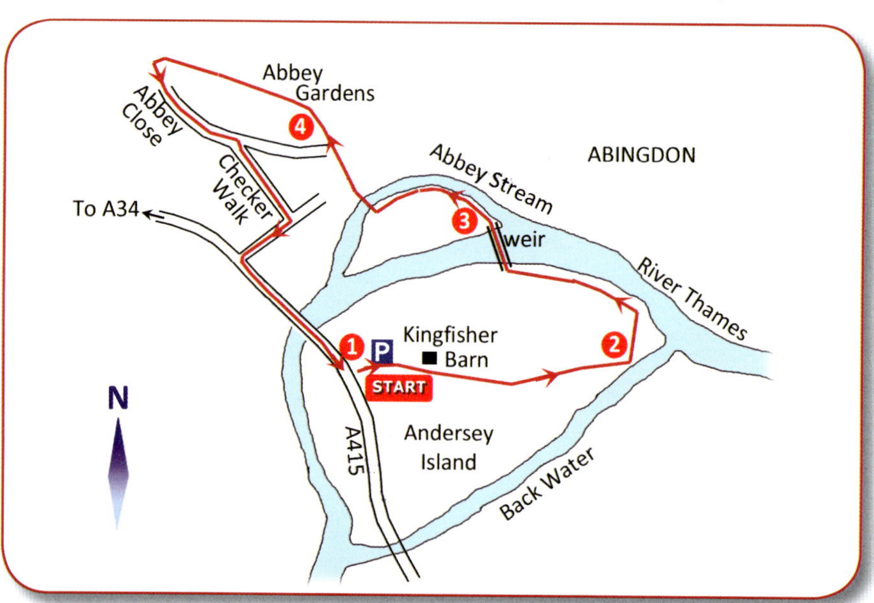

Abingdon and the River Thames

Watching the boats on the River Thames.

there are sweeping views over the trees and fields of Andersey Island. Shortly you pass Kingfisher Barn on your left and a couple of cottages. Walk by the side of a metal farm gate and continue ahead along an earth track. Cross a small footbridge into a meadow, filled with wild flowers in summer. Follow the path across the field heading towards some trees. You can see the tops of the boats on the Thames to your left.

2 Turn left at the edge of the field to walk towards the Thames,

◆ Fun Things to See and Do ◆

Younger children will enjoy spending time in **Abbey Meadows play area**, towards the end of the walk. There are also plenty of boats to watch on the Thames, and keep your crusts handy from the picnic to feed the ducks in Abbey Stream. Older children could explore the history of Abingdon in **Abingdon Museum** and the **Abbey Gardens**.

then turn left again and walk back towards Abingdon, with the river directly on your right. Pass a gate with a private fishing sign and continue ahead until you get to Abingdon Lock. By a lock cottage with some flood signs at the door, turn right and cross the weir with care.

3 Continue ahead along a shady path with Abbey Stream on your right. This is a lovely spot with ducks, coots, swans and the occasional heron to look for in the water. Shortly you will see tennis courts on your right and a gate leading into the Abbey Meadows play area, a perfect spot for a rest. By the Abbey Meadows outdoor pool at the edge of the play area, turn right across the bridge and walk ahead into Abbey Gardens.

4 Turn left and follow the path, walking past an impressive statue of Queen Victoria. At the end of the gardens, you see Abingdon Town Council and Tourist Information on your right. You could continue ahead here to have a look round the town. However, to finish the walk, turn immediately left, then right down Checker Walk. This narrow road has cobbled pavements and leads you past medieval Abingdon Abbey and the Unicorn Theatre on your left. You could go through the arched gate to have a look at the hall and garden. Continue through a narrow passage to Thames Street. Turn right and walk down the road, with Abbey Stream on your left, then turn left and walk over Abingdon Bridge. The bridge is over 550 years old and gives you a wonderful view back over the Thames and the walk you have just done. The car park is on your left.

◆ Background Notes ◆

A custom unique to Abingdon is **throwing fruit buns** from the roof of the 17th-century County Hall to celebrate special occasions and royal events. Crowds of people gather in Market Square below to catch the falling buns. The first recorded bun throwing was in 1761, at the coronation of King George III, and the most recent was in 2011, for the wedding of HRH Prince William to Kate Middleton. Abingdon Museum has a display of buns used in the last seventeen bun throwing events.

Wittenham Clumps

On Top of the World

Wittenham Clumps is the name of two chalk hills, Castle Hill and Round Hill, both of which are crowned with ancient beech trees. From the tops of these hills you have a stunning view across south Oxfordshire. This walk takes you to the top of Round Hill, then through Church Meadow, by the banks of the Thames. Wildflower seeds have been sown in this traditional hay meadow to encourage a diversity of plants and insects. Little Wittenham Wood is full of birdsong and is a perfect spot for children to build a den or watch the birds from the hide. From the woods, the walk heads up to Castle Hill, past a beech tree with a poem carved into its trunk by the local Victorian poet, Joseph Tubb. Spend some time on Castle Hill, exploring the curved ramparts of an Iron Age hill fort, before heading back down the hill to the car park.

Getting there Follow the B4016 north out of Didcot, then turn right and follow the road into Little Wittenham. Look out for a brown sign for Project Timescale and take this narrow access road on your left. The car park is on the right with a sign for Little Wittenham Clumps.

Length of walk 1½ miles
Time 2 hours
Terrain There is a steep gradient up to the hills. The walk follows grass and woodland paths.
Start/Parking The free car park at Little Wittenham (GR SU567923).
Map OS Explorer 170 Abingdon, Wantage & Vale of White Horse

Refreshments There are benches at the top of Round Hill where you can sit and admire the sweeping view. Alternatively, visit Poem Tree Café at the Earth Trust Centre in Little Wittenham.

The Walk

1 Go through the car park gate, passing a relief map of the area and distinctive Earth Trust post. Take the steep grassy path ahead of you up to Round Hill. The path skirts round the western edge of the hill to a trig point with the most amazing view. Follow the path down towards St Peter's church in Little Wittenham, passing a metal gate at the bottom of the hill to reach an Earth Trust post and map. You could take a detour at this point to explore the church and spot

◆ Fun Things to See and Do ◆

There are five different species of **bat** living in Little Wittenham Wood. See if you can spot any bat boxes fixed to the trees. Look out for the tracks of badgers, deer and fox in wet mud and visit the **bird hide** where you might be lucky enough to spot kingfishers or an otter by the river. There are also lots of branches on the ground where you could **build yourself a den**. Try packing fallen leaves between the branches. Do you think you could make your den waterproof? The top of Round Hill is the perfect spot to **fly a kite**.

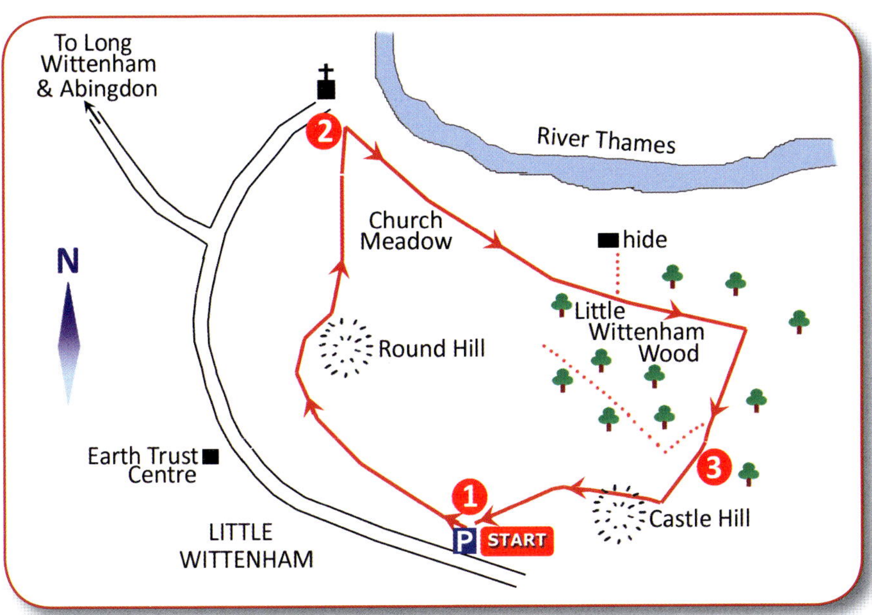

its 'Ace of Spades' window, paid for by a local merchant with a lucky win.

2 From the post, the walk crosses diagonally over Church Meadow towards Little Wittenham Wood, with the Thames on your left. Follow this grassy path until you come to a gate which takes you into the wood. Continue ahead, passing blackberry bushes. The path on the left leads to the bird hide, but to stay on the main walk continue ahead until you take a path on your right opposite a clearing and a bench. The wood

Den building in Little Wittenham Wood.

Kiddiwalks in Oxfordshire

here is fenced off either side of the path to protect orchids from hungry deer. When the path forks, go left and walk out of the wood for about 100 yards and into an arable field, passing an Earth Trust post on your right.

3 Turn right and follow the edge of the field gently uphill. Pass a metal gate on your right and keep ahead towards Castle Hill. Take the path at the top of the hill straight on to the edge of a hedgerow. Go through a metal gate to the ramparts and ditch of Castle Hill fort, where the banks are decorated with cowslips in spring. Turn right and walk up the steep slope. Walk across the wide, grassy plateau towards a large boulder. On one side of the boulder is a poem, copied in 1965 from that carved into the poem tree behind you in 1844–45 by Joseph Tubb. Continue ahead to walk round the top of Castle Hill. There are views on your left across the Sinodun Hills towards Brightwell Barrow. Soon you will see Didcot Power Station ahead. A gravel path leads you back to the path you took at the start of the walk, and the car park.

◆ Background Notes ◆

Wittenham Clumps have been owned and managed by **Earth Trust** since the early 1980s. This is an environmental charity which aims to reconnect people with nature and educate them about the importance of the natural environment. The Earth Trust Centre, in the nearby village of Little Wittenham, has more information about other places to visit and their events. Earth Trust holds popular **lambing weekends** in March and April, with craft activities and the chance to see new-born lambs. The **Children's Food Festivals** are designed to turn fussy eaters into foodies by giving children an opportunity to handle ingredients and find out about real food. The first Children's Food Festival was held in 2007, with Raymond Blanc and Sophie Grigson as patrons. The Trust also organises unique **Green Birthday Parties** at Wittenham Clumps, where your child can create magnificent sculptures using natural materials, go pond dipping, build a shelter or have a fairies tea party. The Earth Trust website has more information about its work and ethos, visit www. earthtrust.org.uk

Watlington Hill

Raptors and Rare Butterflies

A panoramic view from the top of Watlington Hill.

Watlington Hill is maintained by the National Trust, as well as hundreds of rabbits, who nibble the grass, and sometimes the wild flowers that create the perfect habitat for butterflies. There are muntjac and fallow deer in the woods, while the graceful red kites soar and wheel in the sky above. As you sit on the top of the hill, you have the most amazing view over the rolling Chilterns, a designated Area of Outstanding Natural Beauty since 1965. This walk follows the summit of the hill down to the White Mark, before heading back along an ancient sunken path, past yew trees and native woodland.

Getting there From junction 6 of the M40, head south on the B4009 for about 4 miles to Watlington. Take the first left onto Hill Road, passing the Carriers Arms and heading for Christmas Common. The car park is at the top of this road on the right, opposite Watlington Hill Farm.

Length of walk 1¾ miles
Time 1½ hours
Terrain Woodland paths and springy turf on Watlington Hill. A short, steep downhill section.
Start/Parking Watlington Hill NT car park (GR SU711935).
Map OS Explorer 171 Chiltern Hills West

A photo call at the woods.

◆ Fun Things to See and Do ◆

Children can race up and down the sides of the hill and search the many rabbit holes for signs of life. From the top of the hill, you can often spot the red kite which is easily distinguished by its forked tail and reddish feathers. Other **birds of prey** you might see include Britain's commonest raptor, the kestrel, and the sparrowhawk, which has a long barred tail and shorter, more rounded wings than the kite.

Summer brings **wild flowers** to the slopes of the hill. If you see a star-shaped cluster of tiny lilac flowers, it is the rare Chiltern gentian, which is only found in this area. More common but no less pretty are rock roses, while in June, you can see the spiked flower heads of the spotted and bee orchids.

Watlington Hill is also the perfect place for children to do some **butterfly spotting**. The rare silver-spotted skipper lays its eggs here and can be seen in large numbers in August. This butterfly looks quite moth-like, with brown wings lightened with silvery-white spots, which is how it gets its name. It can only be found on chalk downland in the south of England. The brown argus is another butterfly that lives in this part of the country. This butterfly is prettier than its name, with orange spots along the edges of its wings. A bright green butterfly is the green hairstreak and on the south slope you might be lucky enough to see a chalkhill blue which, as its name suggests, is blue and only lives on the chalkland of southern England.

Refreshments The top of the hill is the perfect spot for a picnic, with the occasional bench dotted along the top of the ridge. The Fox and Hounds in Christmas Common is five minutes away by car, and welcomes children, dogs and muddy boots. This 17th-century pub has a good quality children's menu and serves food every lunchtime (☎ 01491 612599).

The Walk

1 Follow the footpath from the car park, between the information signs. Walk straight on through the woods past a National Trust sign on your right, and continue ahead. Then go through a gate which leads you onto Watlington Hill. Walk along the top of the hill, admiring the view from the north-facing slope over the Chilterns to your right, then walk through patches of scrub and gorse. Head downhill and veer to the right, walking towards Watlington, to see the White Mark. There is a bench at the top of the mark, and you can see from this point how the mark lines up with the church below you. Walk steeply downhill past the chalk mark to a metal gate. Go through the gate and cross the stile on your left.

2 Follow a narrow path through the trees, watching out for rabbit holes in the middle of the path. As the path leads uphill and out of the trees, head for the yew wood which you can see ahead of you. Follow the path that runs just below the wood. This path

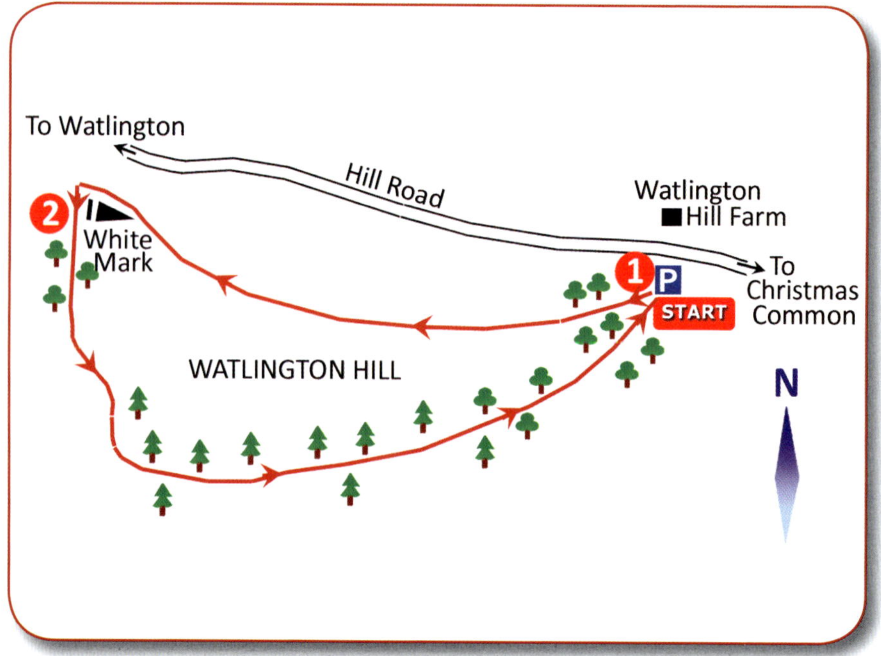

eventually leads you back into the woods and down four wooden steps. Turn left to follow the sunken path through ancient yew trees, heading east. Go through a metal kissing gate and continue through the woods to a gate, then follow the footpath back to the car park.

◆ Background Notes ◆

The native **red kite** became extinct in England and Scotland at the end of the 19th century due to egg collectors, as well as gamekeepers and farmers, who considered it to be vermin. After its reintroduction in 1989 by the Nature Conservancy Council and the RSPB, surely no one could have predicted just how well the magnificent red kite would do in the Chilterns. The new birds were brought from northern Spain and were initially placed in wooden release pens on the Oxfordshire/Buckinghamshire border, where they were observed and health checked, before being released into the wild. The first successful breeding in the Chilterns was in 1992, and now there are over 500 breeding pairs. The programme has been so successful, that Chilterns chicks are being used for reintroduction projects in other parts of England and Scotland, while Welsh kites are being introduced in Northern Ireland.

More than 100 million years ago, the **chalk rock** that forms the Chilterns, lay on the ocean floor. Layers of marine sediment built up and as the earth's tectonic plates shifted, this chalk rock was lifted and folded into the gentle, undulating hills that you see around you.

Watlington White Mark was cut into the hill in 1764 by Edward Horne, and was made by removing the turf to expose the white chalk beneath. The story says that he thought Watlington church would look better with more than just a tower, so he cut the triangular shape into the hill. Looking from the other side of the church in Watlington, the tower now looks as if it is topped with a tall spire.

Greys Court Estate

Ancient Beechwoods in the Chiltern Hills

Set in the heart of the rolling Chilterns is the 16th-century manor house of Greys Court. This walk explores the ancient beechwoods and open glades that surround the house. The woods are a rich habitat for wildlife with the sound of birdsong and the wind in the treetops, while the occasional deer darts through the trees. The estate is owned by the National Trust and is free to walk through, although you will have to pay if you want to visit Greys Court. The walk passes right by the gates of this manor house and gardens and they are well worth exploring, with a 12th-century Great Tower to climb, a series of small walled gardens and a rare Tudor donkey wheel.

Getting there From Caversham, follow the B481 north through Sonning Common to Bolt's Cross, where you take the right turn to Greys Green, then turn left for Greys Court. From Henley-on-Thames, follow the signs for Badgemore Golf Club, heading west out of town, then continue along the same road for just over a mile, to reach Greys Court on your right.

Length of walk 2 miles
Time 1½ hours
Terrain Field and woodland paths with some steeper sections. There are some steps in the woods and large tree roots which would make it hard to push a buggy. No dogs allowed in the NT gardens.
Start/Parking From April to October, park in Greys Court NT car park. The walk starts on the public footpath at the top of the car park (GR SU725833). In winter, park in the lay-by on the southern end of Rocky Lane and follow the public footpath sign through the car park to start the walk.
Map OS Explorer 171 Chiltern Hills West
Refreshments There are picnic tables by the car park. Greys Court tea room and the NT shop are open from April to October. The shop sells sweets, biscuits and ice cream.

The Walk

1 Walk up to the top of the car park and go through a gate, passing some picnic tables on your right. Follow the path straight on and through a gate.

Kiddiwalks in Oxfordshire

on your right. Go through a gate into a field then straight through the next gate on your left. This grassy footpath takes you past farm buildings to a track, with Park Cottage on your right. Cross the track and go through a swing gate into a large field. Follow the path across the field and under the telephone lines, to a gate at the far side. Go through the kissing gate into a beautiful area of ancient beech woodland. In spring, this woodland floor is carpeted with bluebells.

2 Turn left and follow the woodland path, with just the sound of the leaves underfoot and the wind in the trees above you. These woods are full of deer so keep an eye out and you might be lucky and spot one darting through the trees. Follow the edge

After about 80 yards, go through a gate on your left, opposite a massive felled tree. Follow the path over a small footbridge, with a wire fence and pond beyond it

◆ Fun Things to See and Do ◆

The National Trust has a programme of **family events** in the spring and summer at Greys Court. For more information, as well as admission prices and opening times, look on the website: http://beta.nationaltrust.org. uk/greys-court/. They also provide an **explorer pack, and garden and house trails** for children. In the **woods**, children can look for deer, listen to the distinctive hammering of green woodpeckers and the call of the cuckoo in spring, build dens, climb trees, play on the rope swings and pick blackberries.

of the wood with fields on your left, until you see white arrows on the tree trunks where the path veers slightly to the right. Look out for a gate on your left, which leads you off the public bridleway and onto a National Trust footpath.

3 Stay on this path as it meanders through Pissen Wood and down some steps. When you come to a fork in the path, turn left, keeping the post with a 7 on your right. At the end of the path, just before a farm gate leading to Rocky Lane, turn left and walk uphill, past an 8 post, or if you have parked on Rocky Lane, go through the gate to your car. The path leads through the woods and some dense rhododendron bushes until you suddenly emerge from the woods onto the drive of Greys Court. Turn left, passing the entrance to Greys Court, to return to the car park.

◆ Background Notes ◆

Beechwoods are a characteristic feature of the Chilterns. The wood was used to make furniture, with High Wycombe the capital of the chair-making trade in the 19th century, where the famous Windsor chair was produced. Pit-sawyers would dig a deep pit to cut the felled trunks into planks, with a double-handled saw. The lucky 'top dog' stood on top of the pit, while the unfortunate 'under dog' sawed from below, with his eyes and lungs filling with sawdust. You can sometimes find these overgrown pits in the woods.

Coppicing is a form of woodland management that guaranteed a regular supply of timber for fuel and the furniture trade. In the latter half of the 20th century, many coppice woodlands were cut down for agriculture or planted with conifers. However, a managed coppice woodland is hugely beneficial to wildlife and the National Trust are continuing the practice in Pissen Wood. A newly-cut coppice allows light and warmth onto the woodland floor, which helps woodland flowers and insects. A thicket of shrubs grows and then thrives in the sunlight, providing a habitat for ground-nesting birds, small mammals and insects. Managed coppicing provides a cycle of different habitats, as the species which prefer the light and warmth of bare ground move to a recently coppiced area.

Mapledurham

A Mysterious Statue and Hidden Tunnels

The walk returns through Park Wood.

This walk starts in the picturesque village of Mapledurham which is dominated by the Elizabethan Mapledurham House, ancestral home to the Blount family since the end of the 15th century. You follow a well-surfaced estate road, with impressive views over the fields towards the Thames and Mapledurham House, before heading uphill to Park Wood, where bluebells carpet the woodland floor in spring. There is a more unexpected find in the woods, where you can discover a statue on a red brick plinth, peeping over the tops of the surrounding yew trees.

Mapledurham

Getting there From the A4074 heading from Oxford, turn right about 2 miles before Caversham, by the Pack Saddle pub, then turn left following the brown tourist sign to Mapledurham House and the watermill. Drive with care for a mile down this single track road to the village.

Length of walk 2 miles
Time 1½ hours
Terrain Concrete estate roads, fields and woodland paths. Some up and downhill sections and stiles.

Start/Parking There are some spaces for careful parking in the village, making sure you avoid yellow lines and residents' drives. There is a small car park by St Margaret's church, although avoid times when a service is being held. The walk starts on the bridleway opposite The Mill House, at the northern edge of the village (GR SU672768).
Map OS Explorer 159 Reading
Refreshments There are tea rooms in Mapledurham House, or you could bring a picnic to eat on the walk. The nearby Pack Saddle pub serves food every day, using locally sourced ingredients. It has a children's play area and large beer garden (☎ 0118 9463000).

The Walk

1 Follow the Chilterns Way signed '1½ miles to Gravel Hill', passing a post box and phone box on your right. Shortly, you can see Mapledurham House across the lawns to your right, while there are cows in the fields on your left. Pass Park Farm on your left which is a dairy farm. Continue ahead until

93

you come to a choice of paths, with New Lodge Cottage on your left.

2 Turn left here and walk past a grain store on your right. The path then veers to the left and

Mapledurham House near the start of the walk.

leads gradually uphill to follow the edge of Park Wood. Continue along this path until it leaves Park Wood behind for about 100 yards, walking with fields either side of you. At the end of this path turn left and cross the stile on your left into the field.

3 Follow the Chiltern Way across this field to another stile opposite you. Then follow the footpath through Park Wood, heading west. Pass a yellow arrow showing the route of the footpath and continue ahead and slightly downhill to some

◆ Fun Things to See and Do ◆

In Park Wood, children can discover the **mysterious statue** and wonder who it is and why it was built there. Some people think it is a statue of Pan, the Greek god of goats, sheep and shepherds. Pan had the face and body of a man with the legs and tail of a goat. He used to wander the mountains of Arcadia playing his pan pipes. There is a story that the 18th-century poet, Alexander Pope, who was in love with Martha Blount from Mapledurhum House, had the statue built for her. Another story is that the statue is Old Palm and that he is holding a jug and represents the River Thames. There are also tales that on Christmas Eve, Old Palm climbs down from his pedestal and makes his way through the woods to the village of Mapledurham, to wish everyone a Merry Christmas. There are also rumours of secret passageways leading from near the statue to Mapledurham House. The Blounts, who owned Mapledurham House, were Catholics. Catholics were persecuted during the Elizabethan and Stuart periods and they could be locked up and have their money and property confiscated. Mapledurham House has a priest hole, which was a secret place where a visiting priest could hide from the king's soldiers.

blackberry bushes. Turn left onto a wider open path then almost immediately right. This path weaves past bracken and blackberry bushes, passing the brick plinth topped with a statue on your right. Continue ahead as the path passes downhill past another yellow arrow. Cross a stile and walk ahead across the field to another stile and the concrete track you walked along at the start of the walk. Turn right and retrace your steps back to your car. If you turn left and walk to the other end of the village, you could visit Mapledurham House.

◆ Background Notes ◆

Mapledurham House and Watermill are open at weekends and bank holidays from Easter Saturday until the end of September. Their website gives more details of opening times and a detailed history of the house (www.mapledurham.co.uk). The watermill is the last working mill on the Thames. Wheat from the surrounding fields is ground by the old millstones and turned into wholemeal flour which you can buy in the watermill shop.

Although it is just a few miles north of Reading, the **village of Mapledurham** can only be reached by car on a narrow winding country lane. This remote location has preserved the village in its own time capsule, with no modern development to spoil its tranquillity. It is worth spending a little time at the end of the walk to explore the village and admire its pretty cottages and St Margaret's church. The south aisle dates from the 13th century, and inside you can see the tombs of local nobility, one topped with a magnificent brass engraving. On the church walls you can see the coats of arms of various noblemen. The unspoilt nature of the village has made it popular as a film location. The 1976 film *The Eagle has Landed* starring Michael Caine, was filmed in the church, Mapledurham House and the watermill. The fee for using the location was spent on repairing the mill, which had fallen into disrepair after the Second World War.